Frontispiece Pina Bausch performing in *Café Müller* (1978). Photo by Bettina Stöß

PINA BAUSCH

Routledge Performance Practitioners is a series of introductory guides to the key theater-makers of the last century. Each volume explains the background to and the work of one of the major influences on twentieth- and twenty-first-century performance.

This book is the first English-language overview of Pina Bausch's work and methods, combining:

- an historical and artistic context for Bausch's work
- her own words on her work, including a newly published interview
- a detailed account of her groundbreaking work *Kontakthof*, as performed by Tanztheater Wuppertal and by ladies and gentlemen over 65
- practical exercises derived from Bausch's working method for artists and students of both dance and theater.

As a first step towards critical understanding, and as an initial exploration before going on to further, primary research, **Routledge Performance Practitioners** are unbeatable value for today's student.

Royd Climenhaga currently teaches at Eugene Lang College/The New School University in New York City. He writes on intersections between dance and theater and develops and produces new physical performance works as Co-Artistic Director of Human Company.

ROUTLEDGE PERFORMANCE PRACTITIONERS

Series editor: Franc Chamberlain, University College Cork

Routledge Performance Practitioners is an innovative series of introductory handbooks on key figures in twentieth- and twenty-first-century performance practice. Each volume focuses on a theater-maker whose practical and theoretical work has in some way transformed the way we understand theater and performance. The books are carefully structured to enable the reader to gain a good grasp of the fundamental elements underpinning each practitioner's work. They will provide an inspiring springboard for future study, unpacking and explaining what can initially seem daunting.

The main sections of each book cover:

- personal biography
- explanation of key writings
- description of significant productions
- reproduction of practical exercises.

Volumes currently available in the series are:

Eugenio Barba by Jane Turner
Pina Bausch by Royd Climenhaga
Augusto Boal by Frances Babbage
Bertolt Brecht by Meg Mumford
Michael Chekhov by Franc Chamberlain
Jacques Copeau by Mark Evans
Etienne Decroux by Thomas Leabhart
Jerzy Grotowski by James Slowiak and Jairo Cuesta
Anna Halprin by Libby Worth and Helen Poyner
Rudolf Laban by Karen K. Bradley
Jacques Lecoq by Simon Murray
Robert Lepage by Aleksandar Dundjerovic
Joan Littlewood by Nadine Holdsworth
Vsevolod Meyerhold by Jonathan Pitches
Ariane Mnouchkine by Judith G. Miller

PINA BAUSCH

Royd Climenhaga

LONDON AND NEW YORK

First published 2009
by Routledge
2 Park Square, Milton Park, Abingdon, Oxon OX14 4RN

Simultaneously published in the USA and Canada
by Routledge
270 Madison Avenue, New York, NY 10016

Routledge is an imprint of the Taylor & Francis Group, an informa business

Typeset in Perpetua by
Taylor & Francis Books
Printed and bound in Great Britain by
TJ International Ltd, Padstow, Cornwall

British Library Cataloguing in Publication Data
A catalogue record for this book is available from the British Library

Library of Congress Cataloging in Publication Data
A catalog record for this book has been requested

ISBN10: 0-415-37521-5 (hbk)
ISBN10: 0-415-37522-3 (pbk)
ISBN10: 0-203-09895-1 (ebk)

ISBN13: 978-0-415-37521-4 (hbk)
ISBN13: 978-0-415-37522-1 (pbk)
ISBN13: 978-0-203-09895-0 (ebk)

CONTENTS

FIGURES

Photographs by Bettina Stöß, see www.moving-moments.de

Photographs by Jean-Louis Fernandez from *Kontakthof: A Piece by Pina Bausch, with Ladies and Gentlemen over 65*; published by Tanztheater Wuppertal and La Comedie de Clermont Ferrand, available at: www.lacomediedeclermont.com

ACKNOWLEDGMENTS

I would especially like to thank Pina Bausch, not only for her work, but for her warmth and graciousness whenever we met. I made several trips to Wuppertal while researching this book and the staff at Tanztheater Wuppertal was extremely helpful. Mattheis Schmiegelt, Oliver Golloch, and Ursula Propp all provided assistance in accessing video archives and tracking down permission for using the interview with Ruth Berghaus. Thanks to company member Dominique Mercy for his willingness to talk with me as well.

I was able to see Bausch's work live at several venues across America and Europe, but the Brooklyn Academy of Music (BAM) was my primary stop over the last twenty-five years and I want to thank them for their continued championing of Bausch and innovative performance from around the world. The staff at the German Dance Archive in Cologne was very helpful on my visits there.

Thanks to Ellen Cremer for her fluid and elegant translation work and to Vida Midgelow for her extremely useful comments on the practical exercises section of the book. At Routledge, Franc Chamberlain provided excellent editorial advice throughout and was patient and kind as I worked through my own difficulties, and I want to thank Talia Rodgers for her interest in my work and for helping to pass it along to this series.

I have received so much support over the years to pursue my interest in Bausch's work, and to bring out my writing. Thanks to Sondra Fraleigh for reading my writing on Bausch and for her support and encouraging Routledge to consider my work. Thanks too to Anne Bogart for her continual support, encouragement, and comments on my Bausch writing. Lynn Blom provided initial advice, support, and love as I first wrestled with both how to write about Bausch's process and how I might use what I learned in my own performance work. Leland Roloff always inspired me to keep going as I attempted to get my thinking about Bausch into serviceable form, and Roger Copeland provided the impetus that sent me down the path of my interest in Bausch's work.

Thanks to Brooks Hill and Trinity University for travel and research funds to help support this project and to the RF Johnson research fund at Connecticut College. I'd also like to thank my colleagues and especially my students at both those schools and at my current home, Eugene Lang College, The New School for the Liberal Arts. I have refined the ideas in this book in the class room, the rehearsal hall, and on stage over the last several years, and my students always provided a clear voice on what worked and what didn't.

I am so fortunate to have a loving and supportive family and network of friends who have helped in innumerable ways as I work to develop my art and make it a part of my life. Finally, Kelly Hanson provides love and support on every level, emotional, creative, and critical. She offers me everything and my gratitude is immense.

1

AN ARTISTIC AND
CONTEXTUAL HISTORY

THE GROUND

Pina Bausch's piece *Kontakthof* (1978) begins with the performers all simply walking downstage. They move in a group, walking in rhythm with a purposeful hip thrust and slouch, reach the edge of the stage and return upstage to move toward the audience again. Then the group gathers, glaring out at us, before they begin coming forward one at a time. Each performer looks out at the audience, then turns and shows us his or her profile, then turns again to show his or her back. They bare their teeth, or pull up a skirt or pant leg to reveal a well-toned leg. The effect is oddly unsettling, a presentation of self as if for sale, calling attention to the engagement of self in the mating ritual to come and of the ground of the theater itself. We have, after all, paid our money to look at these people, to watch them display their wares for the next three-plus hours, and their looks back at the audience make us deeply aware of our own implication in the process.

This moment from an early work by Bausch and her company, Tanztheater Wuppertal, is emblematic of a dramatic change of approach in the world of dance, and a great call toward new possibility in theater. Never before had someone so clearly and succinctly exposed the inner workings of the stage as a means of engagement and display,

and used that uncovering for immediate visceral impact. It is a pure moment of performance that reflects back upon the audience and makes us aware of our own complicity in taking in the worlds that are presented for us. Epic theater pioneer Bertolt Brecht (1898–1956) had certainly played with the artifice of performance for effective purpose, and he drew on similar influences in the dance world, where German expressionist dancers expressed that self-conscious presence through the performers' bodies. But here we have a culmination of theatrical questioning posed against the physical dimensions of each performer's presence. Dance is uncovered and theater is pushed in a new direction as the two forms are merged into a seamless whole. A new form is created, which critics begin to label "tanztheater" or dance-theater. No longer are we telling a theatrical story through dance movement or playing out characters in a drama through physical action. The theatricality of the moment is enacted on the bodies of the performers themselves.

Just a year before the premiere of this piece, when asked how she selects dancers for her company, Bausch famously replied: "I'm not so interested in how they move as in what moves them" (quoted in Schmidt 1984: 15–16). It has become a defining statement for Bausch's work. Here was work that was going to be based not in technique (although all of her performers bring years of training and often amazing technique to the process of creating her works), but on the emotional ground of the performers themselves, on what made them most human. This is a departure from conventional, movement-based dance forms, especially from the increasingly formalist stance of dance in America at the time, but not that out of line for someone who grew up in a German dance structure working to reconcile itself with its expressionist past. It also has within it traces of the more emotive dance structures Bausch had encountered in America along with combinations of German theatrical traditions going back to cabaret provocations from the early twentieth century, and the raw, visceral quality of experimental theater Bausch experienced in New York in the early 1960s.

Bausch had begun to explore new ideas on stage in her first pieces with Tanztheater Wuppertal in 1975 and 1976, but she realizes the difference of her approach while developing works like *Kontakthof* in the late 1970s. In an interview with Jochen Schmidt in 1978, she said:

> We're still not doing what we really want to do … I think we're all still holding
> back. It's quite natural because after all we want to be loved and liked. And I
> think there is something that holds you back somewhere. You think that this is
> the point and if you go beyond then there's no exact telling where it will lead.
>
> (Bausch 1978: 230)

The need to move past previous forms, to find a new way of telling, is present here, but the real break from conventional dance may have come a few years earlier.

Bausch was working on *The Seven Deadly Sins* and *Don't Be Afraid* (1976), both based on material Brecht created with his frequent musical collaborator Kurt Weill (1900–50). In these early works, Brecht was experimenting with that self-conscious artifice that would seem to suit Bausch's developing style. But in the middle of rehearsals, Bausch says, "something happened between the company and me. For the first time I was afraid of my dancers. They hated the work. They would not understand or accept it. Once, at the end of rehearsal, Vivienne Newport shouted out violently, 'Enough! I can't take it anymore! All of this, I hate it!'" (quoted in Finkel 1991: 5).

What happened in that moment? What were the dancers reacting against, and how did a response to that push the idea of both dance and theater in new directions? Answering those questions requires some understanding of the contextual ground on which Bausch stood, and which she was overturning. In this chapter, I will explore that process of transformation within the progression of Bausch's own work, as well as tracing those influences back into the motivating factors in both dance and theater that set the tone for the ground-breaking work to come. Finally, I will follow Bausch's own influence through the performance world and begin to trace the impact her work has had on a new generation of artists challenging the boundaries of performance practice.

PINA BAUSCH: LIFE AND WORK

BAUSCH'S PERSONAL HISTORY AND DANCE IN GERMANY AND AMERICA

Pina Bausch was born in Solingen, Germany in 1940. She still maintains her dancer's rail-thin frame on which she glides through a room. She often has a rather intense expression on her face, and frequently a

cigarette dangling from her fingers, but quickly erupts into a broad smile when considering an idea. She chooses her words carefully and hides her intelligence and creativity behind an unassuming graciousness. Intensely curious, she always appears to be looking at any situation she is in to try to find what is of most value. The moments she stops to consider are most often small interpersonal connections; the little things that reveal a greater sense of the people she meets. It is this driving interest in people, expressed in all their particularity, that funds both her personal interactions and her work.

She was raised in her parents' café, often playing underneath one of the tables and watching the patrons as they played out their social connections, and occasionally, their muted passions in front of her. After an early grounding in ballet, Bausch entered the Folkwang School in Essen in 1955. There she studied with Kurt Jooss, one of the seminal figures in European modern dance. Jooss' work at Folkwang after the war provided one of the few outlets to explore modern dance practice in Germany, and he drew on some of the primary energies that he helped foster in the fervent development of expressionist dance in the 1920s. This is the first base on which Bausch's work and the growth of tanztheater stands.

GERMAN EXPRESSIONIST DANCE: LABAN, WIGMAN, AND JOOSS

Rudolf Laban (1879–1958) is most often cited as the pioneer of modern dance in Germany. While the influences of **Mary Wigman** (1886–1973) and **Kurt Jooss** (1901–79) were large, even they trace their roots to Laban's creative presence. He was interested in the flow and rhythm of the body as a defining factor in dance, and specifically how those elements connected to the spirit of the dancer.

Mary Wigman became a major contributor and collaborator in Laban's studies. Her interests always pushed toward the more personal entrance into the world of dance, while Laban looked for the next great unifying theorem. The goal of Wigman's work, once she left Laban's company to start her own, was to push toward individual expression, and to establish strategies for creating movement that directly evoked feelings rather than pointing at them from the outside. As she says,

> My purpose is not to "interpret" the emotions ... My dances flow
> rather from certain states of being, different states of vitality which
> release in me a varying play of the emotions, and in themselves
> dictate the distinguishing atmospheres of the dances ... Thus on
> the rock of basic feeling I slowly build each structure.
>
> (Wigman 1975: 86)

> In 1926, Kurt Jooss had just left Laban's company and was asked to
> create a dance program for a new school in Essen that would combine
> dance, music and theater. The Folkwang School, as it was called,
> opened in 1927 with Jooss as director of dance. He instituted a program
> based on Laban's theories where individual movement values were
> placed amid an established base in objective structures of presentation, and
> sought a balance between the grand structures of ballet and the free
> expression of modern dance. Jooss created his landmark anti-war
> ballet/dance-theater piece *The Green Table* in 1932 as an attempt to marry
> the two forms, and in response to the cultural conditions he saw around him.

Jooss' teaching at the Folkwang School came out of his early work
with Rudolf Laban. As opposed to a movement technique, Laban sought
to uncover expressive potential in physical presence within groups of
people. In reaction against the ornate surface of classical ballet and
some of Laban's group work with movement choirs, Mary Wigman
looked toward "everyday" movements to develop a working method
that might express personal experience. She emphasized individual
expression through the "ausdrucks-gebarde" or expressive gesture, an
evocative "everyday" movement, developed and stylized to recontextualize and heighten its original intent. The shift from the developed
surface of the classical tradition to a probe into more interior depths
brought with it a move from collective to individual experience. That
redirection of expressive purpose was fully invested in Jooss' work at
the Folkwang School, and is the seed from which Bausch's work and
tanztheater grows.

EARLY EXPERIENCE IN AMERICA

After graduating from the Folkwang School, Bausch went to New
York to study at the Juilliard School. Here she familiarized herself

with the techniques of Martha Graham (1894–1991) and José Limón (1908–72), two of the seminal figures in American modern dance. She was also influenced by her work with Paul Sanasardo, a disciple of the expressive choreographer Anna Sokolow (1910–2000). But perhaps the most vital influence on Bausch during this period was that of Antony Tudor (1908–87). Tudor was one of her instructors at Juilliard, and during the 1961/62 season she danced with the Metropolitan Ballet Theater, then under his direction. Tudor's strongly psychological style, with its emphasis on character built upon emotive gesture, must have reawakened and reconfigured some of Bausch's earlier experiences with emotive gesture in the German dance tradition.

The worlds of American modern dance and ballet were often separate at this time, though Bausch was able to cross more easily between them. Within the modern dance world there were competing aesthetics as well. Graham was the reigning queen of dance at the time, and her technique based on weight and groundedness formed the base from which most American modern dance grew.

AMERICAN MODERN DANCE

Many of the pioneers of American modern dance had worked together in the 1920s and 1930s. Martha Graham had danced in the ground-breaking work of Ruth St. Denis (1879–1968) and Ted Shawn (1891–1972) in the Denishawn company, as did another innovator in American modern dance, Doris Humphrey (1895–1958). Both Graham and Humphrey left to develop their own work and provided one dominant influence before the war. Their work emphasized grand story structures, although both choreographers were looking for ways to leave behind literal interpretations of their work and to push toward a more metaphoric means of presentation.

Another influential thread within the American modern dance mosaic before and immediately after the war was provided by the more emotive styles of dance that were at least partly spurred by energies coming from Europe. Wigman's tours at this point had quite an impact and set the stage for Hanya Holm (1893–1992) to establish the Wigman School in New York. Especially after the war, José Limón and Anna Sokolow also provided new approaches to movement values. Limón had danced with Humphrey's company and Sokolow had been a member of

Graham's. In creating their own work, both dancers emphasized more evocative movement patterns built on emotional structures and divorced from the mythic base of Graham or Humphrey. Sokolow's most important work, *Rooms* (1955), incorporates everyday movements heightened and stylized to reveal psychological states. She developed the piece out of workshop sessions with actors at the Actor's Studio, which was famous for its evocative style of training, and choreographed the movements out of questions she posed to the actors that might reveal inner states. "How does it feel to be near someone who is not there?" (quoted in Warren 1991: 119).

Merce Cunningham (b.1919), another Graham dancer, was also moving outside of the more mythic domain of dance of the 1930s. Graham's own work in the late 1950s and early 1960s was already pushing more toward abstraction, but Cunningham's early work during this period would prove to open the door for the anti-illusionistic postmodern dance to come. Cunningham had been working around boundaries between the arts, particularly in his collaborations with experimental composer John Cage (1912–92), that provided a new way to think about stage presentation based on pure elements of expression. Their pieces utilizing chance and indeterminacy, and their later work collaborating with visual artist Robert Rauschenberg (b.1925), provided one of the influences that led to the wealth of performance experimentation in New York throughout the 1960s.

In addition to her exposure to Tudor- and Graham-based work, when Bausch arrived in New York in 1961 she also had the opportunity to experience a turning of the corner in American modern dance. A new spirit was unfolding away from the mythic influence of the leading lights of the 1930s to new approaches and energies from the other side of the spectrum in more open and abstract work. Bausch was also witness to (or at least in the midst of) a groundswell of new ideas in performance practice and theater. Visual artists were experimenting in performance work called Happenings, and they often worked together with dancers whose formal exercises became the base of the post-modern dance movement.

It is unclear how much of this activity Bausch actually saw or what its overt impact on her might have been, but she could not have helped but feel the spirit of revolution in performance practice that

was going on around her. She has admitted to seeing a performance by the Living Theater, who were incorporating their own reimagining of presentational practice in challenging traditional dramaturgy. Many of the new energies that were taking shape in both the advent of post-modern dance and the growth of experimental theater involved tactics that called attention to the act of performance. The sheer visceral intent of performance, of placing yourself on display for an audience, was uncovered in an attempt to break through codifying structures we may feel inhibited by in everyday life. The experiments were raw and often openly confrontational. Bausch would later use that same unco-vering of visceral presence for precise and subtle purpose. Her time amidst those radical ideas taking shape in New York must have at least opened that potential in her mind. But before Bausch had the oppor-tunity to fully explore the quickly changing landscape of American dance and theater, she was asked back to Germany.

NEW POSSIBILITIES IN GERMANY

In 1962 Bausch took her experiences in dramatic dance technique and experimental presentation back to Germany, where Jooss offered her the position of leading soloist in his Folkwang Ballet. Her dancing with the Folkwang Ballet, under Jooss' direction, was riveting and enigmatic. Hörst Koegler recalls that

> it was through no special will or effort, but just by her very nature that she stood apart from the rest of the dancers. She recalled the women Käthe Kollwitz has drawn; women carrying the burden of generations, who have been exploited through no fault of their own other than having had the misfortune of being born female in a male-dominated society.
>
> (Koegler 1979: 51)

As Germany received support to rebuild its economy following the war, the re-established government invested in a repertory arts pro-gram. All cities were given resources to create theater, opera, sym-phony, art, and ballet centers. While this system ensured widespread development of arts programming throughout Germany, it also tended to emphasize more conservative practice. Modern dance was often overlooked in favor of ballet. German dance was at a crossroads, with the split between entrenched and established conventional ballet

practice and a more upstart exploratory modern movement at its height. Jooss' company provided a rare mixture of ballet structure and some modern technique, and the Folkwang School still offered the most complete and yet progressive approach to dance training. Folkwang provided the means for modern dancers to begin to stake out a claim for their own interests, and to begin working within the repertory system.

Bausch's first work as a choreographer and creator of new pieces began in 1968 after her mentor Kurt Jooss retired. Bausch had been the principal dancer in his Folkwang Ballet but now took over his position at the Folkwang Dance Studio where she began to work out a mixture of dance and theatrical technique. Bausch had worked closely with Jooss for the previous six years and during that time had begun to experiment with new choreography. But Bausch says that this early entrance into choreography came not so much from a desire to create things a certain way as from the simple need to dance. Though tightly constructed, what stood out in these early efforts was Bausch's own emotionally charged attitude. Themes of gender construction and the opposition of the sexes were explored in Bausch's early choreography, setting the tone for the work of her mature period.

The dance world around her at this time was dominated by the parallel influences of George Balanchine (1904–83) in ballet and Merce Cunningham in modern dance. Balanchine brought ballet to its most abstract, moving away from the story structures of earlier classical dance to rely on the power of developed technique and dramatic juxtapositions of formal elements. Cunningham was also concerned with formal values, drawing from the pared down spirit of the post-modern dance movement, and leading the charge away from mythic themes and emotive contexts and toward the potency of pure movement for movement's sake.

Certainly there were a variety of approaches at play in both ballet and post-modern dance, but the overwhelming presence of Balanchine and Cunningham carried considerable weight in America and in Europe, especially Germany, where artistic infrastructures were still recovering from both the physical and cultural devastation of the Second World War. Bausch's early choreographic work recognized these influences, but drew more heavily on the emotive work of her German predecessors.

In 1972 Bausch was asked to choreograph the dances for a production of *Tannhäuser* at the Wuppertal Opera Company. The success

of her unconventional staging led to her being offered the position of director of the Wuppertal Ballet. She accepted the position on the condition that she could bring along many of the dancers with whom she was working at the Folkwang Studio in Essen.

When Bausch first arrived at the newly renamed Tanztheater Wuppertal in 1973, she developed pieces based on set structures. She created pieces based on two operas by Christoph Willibald Gluck (1714–87) (*Iphigenia on Tauris* (1974), and *Orpheus and Eurydice* (1975)) and on Igor Stravinsky's (1882–1971) avant-garde masterpiece from 1913, *Rite of Spring* (1975). But here, rather than following the linear pattern in the original opera or ballet, Bausch took the base condition operating in each story to act as an overriding metaphor from which movement and bodily attitudes grow. Her collage techniques surrounded the ideas to create a multi-faceted perspective of the story, re-creating the condition and mood of each story rather than telling it through a more conventional linear narrative. She drew on her own and her dancers' personal experiences to create presentational movement patterns formed from emotive gestures and derived from a response to, rather than in service of, formal story structures.

Figure 1.1 *Iphigenie auf Tauris* (1974). Photo by Bettina Stöß

The stories are interpreted through present experience. As Bausch states in the yearbook *Ballet 1986*: "I only know that the time in which we live, the time with all its anxieties is very much with me. This is the source of my pieces" (quoted in "Bausch, Pina" 1986: 5). *Rite of Spring*, for instance, returns to Stravinsky's root of a pagan fertility ritual, staging the action from the perspective of the terrified young women who were the potential victims, thus lending it a measure of pity missing in other versions. Bausch is very aware of the plight of women in contemporary society, and the imagery she chooses reflects that concern. In other words, the metaphor of a woman chosen as a sacrifice to the power and control of men is not lost on Bausch, but she is able to extend the metaphor through specific concentration on the motivating impulse of the action, and, therefore, avoid falling into didacticism.

Bausch reduces the ballet down to its most essential image, and concentrates on the depth and power of that motivating image. As she says:

> the most important thing to me was to understand what Stravinsky wanted. In *Rite of Spring*, there is nothing to add to what's already there. There is a young girl, the Chosen One, and that young girl dances, all by herself, until she dies.
>
> (quoted in Finkel 1991: 5)

Bausch continually returns to this technique of concentrating on one essential image or gesture and probing it until it reveals the depth of its associations, its claim to power within the cultural imagination. The initial idea is pushed until even the structural grid which supports it, the foundational impetus for the work, takes on metaphoric value.

These early pieces act as extended explorations of a central idea within an established story and with everything that happens on stage, and the stage itself, working to explore the chosen base operating idea or image. In *Rite of Spring* the stage is covered with peat, which is kicked up lightly at the beginning of the piece but eventually covers the sweat-soaked bodies of the dancers, visibly muddying their white slips until everything is a murky brown. Simply and dramatically the theme of lost innocence slowly builds in the piece through this visual, physical metaphor.

The overriding metaphor for each piece finds expression by whatever means are necessary, whether they be movement based, imagistic, or dramatic, and by employing whatever forms and techniques are

Figure 1.2 *Le Sacre du Printemps* (1975). Photo by Bettina Stöß

available. Bausch began, in this early work, to see the problem before her not as one of choreographing a dance, but as a group of people trying to interpret their experience of an opera or ballet in the rehearsal process and then presenting that experience within an aesthetic structure that develops along with the need to express.

The goal of these early pieces remains, however, to uncover movement patterns that evoke and express the feeling of a piece, and in this way she does not move past more conventional, movement-based notions of dance. The movements she develops, however, draw on the roots of earlier expressionist dance's formulation of the essential emotive gesture, but take on the source of that creation rather than adopting it as an established technique. Bausch returned to the source of everyday actions as they expressed a sense of ourselves as individuals and maintained that individualist stance in performance, rather than mining those actions for movement patterns that are then divorced from the subject to become formal expressions. In *Rite of Spring*, for example, the final sacrificial dance of the virgin is a desperate expression of the fear of the woman going through this ordeal, and the physicality does not point at this fear, but uncovers it through gestural movement structures that begin to break down as the dancer violently throws herself into the exhausting ritual.

Through all of this, while unquestioningly creating riveting pieces, Bausch had not yet ventured past the bounds of what most would firmly consider dance. Her dances were evocative, dramatic, and relied on metaphor and setting as extensions of feeling and character, but were still based squarely on movement as the central impetus of the work, even if that movement was addressed on different terms than other dance at the time.

But something new was afoot. The dancers were asked to push beyond their accustomed role as impersonal movers to bring more of their individual lives to bear on the material and the means of expression. Especially as Bausch moved from the story ballets to the Brecht/Weill material she drew from for *The Seven Deadly Sins* and *Don't Be Afraid* (1976), the dancers were increasingly asked to put themselves in very demanding emotional situations. Bausch was beginning to uncover the very heart of the process of dance, the motivating impulse from which movement begins, and that impulse is always a person in a specific situation.

In *Don't Be Afraid*, as in *Rite of Spring*, the woman who is the chosen victim constantly runs away from the man who pursues her, sweetly singing his song in what we come to understand is an attempt to assuage the rape that is to come. The performer herself is manhandled on stage and continually trapped in positions from which she fights to escape. The physical action is specific, but the expression comes from the performers' entrance into the moment and engagement of the emotions at stake rather than their ability to execute the movement. The pieces as performed were becoming the arrangement of those moments as discovered in rehearsal out of the performers' own experience and presented within physical and dramatic terms. The structure is still built upon a dance ground, but is starting to be expressed with the representational methods of the theater, and the dancer is allowed to show personal openness beyond the degree of her turnout.

As Meryl Tankard recalled her response to the questioning mode of her audition for the company shortly after this period:

> It was the first time a director had encouraged me to project my own person-
> ality on the stage, and it opened a whole new world. I had nothing against
> being a sylph in a tutu and toe-shoes, but the whole classical repertory sud-
> denly seemed like a museum.
>
> (quoted in Galloway 1984: 41)

It is this revelation of subjective experience in Bausch's pieces – derived from and represented through the dancer's body – that is the basis for tanztheater and that provides its break from dance. It is also what led to the crisis described earlier, and the revolt of some of her dancers. Bausch had pushed against the very support of what it means to be a dancer and was entering new territory.

Engaging content through dance forms was not new in Germany, and the student revolts of the late 1960s had politicized many artists. Dancers felt the need to break with more conventional dance structures to try to be more culturally relevant. Out of this environment grew a group of young choreographers, most with ties to the Folkwang School, who reasserted some of the dramatic and expressionistic tendencies of Ausdruckstanz. They began experimenting with several dance influences derived from their German past and many of their experiences in America. They sought a new way to approach the history and social value of their everyday experiences and to reassert the personal into the political sphere. Johannes Kresnik (b.1939) worked as a reformer within the repertory system, first as head of the Bremen Ballet and later as director of the Heidelberg Ballet. His work challenged the isolated world-view of the ballet tradition and opened up the possibility for young choreographers to address personal social involvement. Kresnik's work showed the potential of working through the repertory structure in reimagining the ground of dance, and it was upon this base that the new aesthetic framework of tanztheater was built.

Bausch's early choreography during this period had begun to explore the nature of expression, and in so doing broke down the model of choreography as the arrangement of steps put forth by Balanchine and echoed by Cunningham, with the rest of the dance world following close behind. Rather than beginning with formal concerns of a body arranged under the governing ideas of an established technique, Bausch begins with the individual expression of her dancers who maintain their personal perspective in surrounding an idea with various approaches to its representation. Bausch took the same elements as those explored by American post-modern dancers of the time – collage techniques, pedestrian movement, repetition, and borrowing from other media – but maintained her interest in the subject to arrive not just at a new technique into which the dancer's body as artistic material might be placed, but at a new form in which human experience is expressed in bodily terms.

Tanztheater forms at the conjunction of these formal practices and more subjective concerns, where it attempts to create an expressive arena for the individual human subject. While dance critics debate if what tanztheater offers is actually dance, theater critics are quick to point out its connection to theater history and the ideas of experimental theater artists from Vsevolod Meyerhold (1874–1940?) and Bertolt Brecht to Jerzy Grotowski (1933–99) and Antonin Artaud (1896–1948). Bausch simply took the methods of construction she knew best from her dance background and developed them through theatrical means. In so doing, she utilized those methods and techniques that best suited her ends, eschewing traditional narrative in theater to concentrate on the expression of the human subject, performed in imagistic moments choreographed into an interlacing field of expression centered on a given topic or story.

DISRUPTIVE UNITY IN *BLAUBART* (1977)

Without articulating a specific agenda to remake dance in theatrical terms, Pina Bausch had begun to erode the base of dance as essentially the connection of movement patterns into an evocative whole. The alarmed reaction was not limited to a few of her dancers. While pieces like *Rite of Spring* had been widely admired by critics, they were only begrudgingly accepted by the more conservative audience back in Wuppertal. By the time Bausch was presenting the Brecht/Weill works in the mid-1970s, the public was not ready to accept these newer forms of presentation. Combined with the continued unrest in rehearsals, Bausch claimed she was ready to give up dance: "After the premiere, I had a terrible crisis. I wanted to give up, never work again. I decided to never set foot in a theater again" (quoted in Finkel 1991: 5).

Jan Minarik (who had been with the company from the beginning and only recently retired as a performer, though he still acts as a consultant) convinced Bausch to come back and continue exploring in this new vein. He had his own studio and gathered a small group of dancers to begin experimenting with presentational strategies. They arrived at *Bluebeard – While Listening to a Tape Recording of Béla Bartok's Opera "Duke Bluebeard's Castle"* (1977). The program made no reference to dance, but listed simply scenes in which the solitary, brutal Bluebeard (Jan Minarik) plays out the scenario of the opera which he plays and replays from a tape recorder on a rolling stand. The music

itself takes on the role of a character, which interacts with the other characters as it moves around the stage on its rolling cart. It is as if Bluebeard the man and *Bluebeard* the opera act in violent collaboration against the other characters who are trapped on stage. The mode of presentation in the final version of the piece mixed forms, combining opera, physicalized theater, and dance, into an overarching visceral aesthetic. This piece marks Bausch's entrance into a mature style and develops the form that helps to define tanztheater.

The work on *Bluebeard* disrupted the previous ground on which dance had stood by de-centering movement as the primary means of expressive potential. The piece is physical in the extreme, but the physicality now serves the purpose of laying bare the inner dimensions of character and relationship. It brings together dance and theatrical energies to give us moments in which we are pulled beyond the surface of the movement and enter into the raw emotion underneath. In one chilling image, Bluebeard is seated at the small desk/tape recorder stand on which he continually re-enacts the violent struggle of the story through playing and replaying pieces of the opera. The current wife (originally played by Marlis Alt), who ultimately uncovers the

Figure 1.3 *Bluebeard* (1977). Photo by Bettina Stöß

brutal truth hidden in Duke Bluebeard's castle, lies hidden at his feet. We see a hand emerge and move up Bluebeard's body to caress his cheek. Bluebeard places his hand on top of her head and violently pushes her back down to his feet. The hand emerges again and again he pushes her down. Again and again, faster and faster, the hand traces its pathway across Bluebeard's body to his cheek in a futile attempt to provide tenderness, to seek comfort, and each time it is met with a violent rebuff. The action, though repeated precisely, speeds up to the point that we begin to fear for the actual dancer's safety. And then it stops for a moment and we take a breath, only to see the hand slowly make its way back up Bluebeard's body to his cheek once more.

The movement is precise and highly developed out of emotive gestural patterns, but the effect of the moment does not come wholly out of the quality of the movement, but in the context of both the moment and the sheer viscerality of the theater. We are brought into the vulnerability of the image in part because the performer herself is perceived to be at risk in some way (although the action is carefully developed in rehearsal to minimize any actual danger). We are able to see the tortured relationship of the characters, to feel the connection and desperation they feel, through the immediacy of their stage presence and the way in which we feel along with the woman in the moment. The specificity of the moment opens up the interior dimensions of the characters and the story, but also moves us past *Bluebeard* itself and into a metaphorical connection to sexual relations in general. And the orchestration, or choreography of this and similar moments into a cohesive structure that continues to evoke that deeper metaphor is Bausch's accomplishment in this piece.

A NEW APPROACH – A NEW LABEL: TANZTHEATER

The term "tanztheater" was perhaps first used by Rudolf Laban in the early part of the twentieth century as a way to describe his choric dance rituals of that time (Partsch-Bergsohn 1987: 37). Kurt Jooss was the first to use the term tanztheater in a formal and consistent manner. He sought a new term to differentiate works such as his ground-breaking anti-war ballet/drama *The Green Table* from the overriding aesthetic of the more conventional story ballets presented throughout Germany at the time (Manning 1993: 246). Gerhard

Bohner (1936–92) first called his group "Tanztheater Darmstadt" when he was appointed ballet director of the Darmstadt Theater in 1972. Critic Jochen Schmidt points out that he was probably following the lead set by the "Nederlands Dans Theater," which was influential at the time. A year later Pina Bausch similarly called her company "Tanztheater Wuppertal," and Bohner and Reinhild Hoffmann (b.1943) later called their company "Tanztheater Bremen" when they took over the direction of the Bremen Ballet.

Amongst the newer generation of German choreographers, the transition from using the term "tanztheater" for a company to applying it to the performances of these choreographers is even more tenuous. Schmidt claims:

> Austrian Johannes Kresnik, whose works are the earliest this label would have suited, called his dance pieces "choreographic theater," while Pina Bausch designated her productions "dance evenings" (Tanzabend), "dance operas" or "operettas," before she used the term "piece" [stuck]. (Bausch first used the term piece for her *Kontakthof* in May of 1977.)
>
> (Schmidt 1985: 59)

It wasn't until the late 1970s that "tanztheater" began to be broadly applied not just to many dance companies in Germany, but to the work they were presenting. Norbert Servos maintains:

> [T]he Wuppertal company, under Pina Bausch, was the first to establish the term "tanztheater" – until then occasionally used in the names of dance companies – as a synonym for a new and independent genre. Tanztheater, a mixture of dance and theater modes, opened up a new dimension for both genres. Basically the term stood for a kind of theater that was aiming at something new both in form and content.
>
> (Servos 1984: 19)

This change in nomenclature indicates a recognition amongst both the choreographers and the critics that the work being presented was quantifiably different than what preceded it, and, as such, needed a new term, or in this case a revived old term now given new meaning through specific application.

Even while Bausch's work was making that decisive move toward new means of expression in the late 1970s, others around her were

similarly pushing boundaries and helping to define new possibilities in performance. Gerhard Bohner re-created, and in the process re-established, some of the energy of the Bauhaus works by Oskar Schlemmer (1888–1943). Essentially formal experiments in space, shape, and time, Schlemmer's works questioned the role of the human subject in performance. Johannes Kresnik had already begun exploring his own version of visceral politics in works often based on characters in extremis, from *Romeo and Juliet* (1975) to the poet Sylvia Plath at the brink of suicide (1985). William Forsythe (b.1949), an American transplant, began working with the Frankfurt Ballet and created a series of pieces that pushed beyond more traditional ballet structures to reach toward more expressive internal truths. Susanne Linke (b.1944) and Reinhild Hoffmann, both coming out of the Folkwang School, also developed new approaches toward expressive possibility. Linke's work contrasted the large-scale productions of other German choreographers, many working within the regional system, and often looked back toward more purely expressionist roots in her solo pieces or duets. Hoffmann worked during this period as the co-director of Tanztheater Bremen where she created a series of large-scale imagistic pieces based on more mythic themes.

A portion of the German dance world was reorienting itself toward this new form of expression, and many contributed to the emergence of the form of tanztheater. None, however, was to have the overall impact of Pina Bausch. Jochen Schmidt goes so far as to say:

> She not only deserves much of the credit for the unexpected ascent of West German dance theater to one of the three major forces of New Dance in the world – alongside America's post-modern dance and Japan's Butoh – she engineered it almost single-handedly. It's not mere presumption to say that her aesthetic sway in the world of contemporary dance is greater than that of any other choreographer today.
>
> (Schmidt 1990: 40)

Her impact is far ranging, both in terms of the many who follow in her footsteps and as it is felt in other dance and theater practices throughout the world. Whenever tanztheater is discussed, Bausch's name inevitably follows. On another occasion Schmidt comments, "It was she who made tanztheater. Without her success, which was not an

easy success, there would not have been tanztheater" (quoted in Daly 1986: 46).

Beyond Schmidt's ardent support, Bausch also generates the same response from other choreographers in the field, most notably Reinhild Hoffmann and Susanne Linke, who both credit her work as the break that allowed their own work to develop and be seen in a new light. (For specific reference, see "Tanztheater," an unpublished transcript from the discussion on tanztheater held at the Lincoln Center Library for the Performing Arts, October 28, 1989.) All three were trained at the Folkwang School in Essen and credit Kurt Jooss with much of the work that set the stage for the development of tanztheater. But it was Bausch, both as a teacher – she took over the head of the Folkwang School from Jooss at the time when Linke was a student, just as Linke took over from Bausch when Hoffmann was a student – and as a choreographer, who paved the way for others to find their own individual paths of expression.

THE DEFINING PERIOD FOR TANZTHEATER, 1977–85

Bausch's challenge and great innovation was to find a way to maintain a dance agenda through choreographic principles of construction while incorporating theatrical techniques of expressing individual subjective experience. This is the point at which dance and theater come together to form tanztheater. Her earlier pieces based on operas or ballets, like *Orpheus and Eurydice* and *Rite of Spring*, already showed that tendency toward subjective engagement through theatrical presence, even while they are still built on choreographed movement patterns established by Bausch as the dominant creator. With *Bluebeard*, she first enters into the questioning process of construction that includes significant input from the ensemble, and that process simultaneously brings with it the subjective presence of the performer and fully integrates a more theatrical presentational structure within the dance form and physical emphasis.

After *Bluebeard*, the company quickly works through several pieces that continue to push at this new formal structure. When she first arrived at Wuppertal, Bausch created pieces more conventionally by developing movement patterns and crafting those on to her ensemble. With *Bluebeard*, she begins with a series of questions and asks the ensemble to find responses. Sometimes the responses take the form of

a performed image, other times it might be a particular movement, and still other times it could be a story the performer might tell. She might ask the performers to describe something lost, or to bring in a precious object, or simply to dance their names. Once those elements are in the room, they may be explored in any way that is appropriate, through words, theatrical images, movement, and so on. The precious object, for instance, may elicit a story, or lead to a scene, or become the impetus for movement. Throughout rehearsals, Bausch watches and takes notes. She asks her performers to write down what they do so that they can remember it and do it again when asked. And she does ask, repeatedly. Moments are tried, expanded upon, linked to other moments, thrown away, and gradually a structure begins to emerge. Each individual response is tied to the underlying question that motivated the piece. *Bluebeard* starts this process, but here the performers are still responding to the cohesive ur-text of the opera. With the next piece, *Komm tanz mit mir* (*Come Dance With Me*, 1977), the base is the company members themselves. The structured exploration of questions takes shape as the underlying formal process of developing the new work and the results include physicality, text, images, sound, and the increasing importance of setting in creating the overall effect of the work on stage.

Despite the time-consuming nature of the process, the company develops and presents two new pieces a year during this period. Bausch works with her partner Rolf Borzik (1944–80) as a designer/ creator of the mise-en-scène throughout this time. Each new piece furthers the process and definition of what tanztheater is and what it might be. Her piece based on *Macbeth* (*He Takes her by the Hand and Leads her into the Castle, the Others Follow* (1978) – the title is derived from a stage direction in *Macbeth*) includes actors in reimagining the presentation. *Café Müller* (1978) is more of a chamber piece for two couples and the lone figure of Bausch herself as a kind of blind dreamer trying to hold on to the fleeting images that are played out before her. In each piece, all the performers are put through the same questioning and rigorous physical process, and each is expected to fully invest in the moment on stage. The pieces develop through collaborative process and in response to the questions at hand. *Kontakthof* (1978) begins with the idea of tenderness. What are the limits of tenderness? When does it move into something else? And from there it moves through a catalogue of the sometimes

humorous, sometimes desperate things we do to each other in our search for connection.

The next phase of this defining period is shaped by two huge personal events in Bausch's life. In 1979 Rolf Borzik is diagnosed with cancer and, early in 1980, dies. His energetic and eclectic personality had been a huge influence on the company, and his personal relationship with Bausch a source of strength. His designs moved past traditional scenography to incorporate the ground of the operating metaphor of the piece, and his role in helping to create pieces would be hard to replace. Bausch begins her collaboration with designer Peter Pabst, with whom she has continued to work on every piece since. Pabst works from a sketch by Borzik to complete *1980 – Ein Stuck von Pina Bausch* (*1980 – A Piece by Pina Bausch*) (1980). The piece becomes a kind of requiem for Borzik, but it is as much a celebration as a remembrance. Built significantly out of images from childhood, there is a sense of lost innocence and a surprising amount of humor. That delicate combination will continue to be the reigning tenor in Bausch's work throughout her career.

The company continues to work, despite the tragedy. In addition to creating new works, they also reprise older pieces for tours and visiting engagements in Europe and Australia. They finally take a break from creating new work in 1981, though their touring schedule at that time must have kept them busy. In the midst of all of this, Bausch gives birth to a son, Rolf Solomon. There is a progression in the work toward lighter material and new themes are explored, but it is too convenient to pin it to that singular event. When the work is built so strongly on the lives of the performers, there are bound to be periods of darkness and light. To me, what Bausch does so effectively is find ways to combine the two. Every moment of despair has room for hope and a bit of laughter, and every lighthearted romp has a serious undercurrent that grounds the work.

The company continues its exploratory process, and continues to define the boundaries of tanztheater. It settles into more of a routine of creating one new work each year and then keeping other works fresh for ever-increasing international tours. In the nine years after the crisis that led to *Bluebeard*, the company reforms and creates fourteen new pieces that establish the ground on which its reputation is based. Many of those early defining pieces are seen in the company's international tours, and Bausch's influence can be felt in the four corners of the dance

world. Dance companies throughout Europe are drawn to this new form of presentation, contributing to new energies in France and an explosion of new dance in Belgium. South American companies are also influenced by a Bausch tour, and Britain gets its first look at the new work in 1982. After an American premiere at the Olympic Arts Festival in Los Angeles in 1984 (to a mostly confused audience) Bausch does two successive seasons at the Brooklyn Academy of Music (BAM) in New York in 1984 and 1985. This period in Bausch's work starts with a hesitant attempt to reimagine what the company might do, and ends with a new form established and its impact felt around the world.

THE COLLISION OF AMERICAN AND GERMAN DANCE

As the formalist post-modern dance movement grew in America, German dance continued to develop along more emotive lines, with choreographers working alongside Bausch to help establish a new tanztheater aesthetic. This new group of German dancers infiltrated the repertory system until, by the mid-1980s, a clear demarcation could be seen between the dominant formalist stance of the body as object and efficator of movement in American dance and the neo-expressionist development of the body as subjective presence in German dance.

The expression of the body as either body-subject or body-object leading toward two distinct avenues of dance practice was perhaps nowhere so evident as in the Next Wave Festival of 1985 at the Brooklyn Academy of Music. There, several tanztheater groups from Germany gave performances that contrasted greatly with the American choreography being presented at BAM and elsewhere in New York at the time. The differences between the German and American work echoed a previous collision of aesthetics when Hanya Holm had brought Mary Wigman's expressionist ideas about dance to New York in the 1930s. Holm explains:

> Emotionally the German dance is basically subjective and the American dance is objective in their characteristic manifestations … The tendency of the American dancer is to observe, portray and comment on her surroundings with an insight into intellectual comprehension and analysis … The German dancer, on the other hand, starts with the actual emotional experience itself and its effect upon the individual.
>
> (quoted in Partsch-Bergsohn and Bergsohn 2003: 57)

The festival at BAM also included a few discussion sections where German and American critics and dancers debated their differences in front of an audience. (For transcripts of these discussion sections, and a collection of other articles on German tanztheater see *TDR*, Spring 1986.) Anna Kisselgoff, as moderator of one of the discussions, set the stage for the confrontation between the two groups by quoting German dance critic Jochen Schmidt:

The New Dance [i.e. post-modern dance] choreographers as we have seen, are interested above all in movement. Pina Bausch, however, has expressly determined that she is less interested in how people move as in what moves them – and that applies, by and large, to her German colleagues Reinhild Hoffmann and Susanne Linke. Whereas the young Americans – inasmuch as they are descendants of the Cunningham–Nikolais generation which defined dance as "motion, not emotion" – are fascinated by dance in itself, their German dance colleagues want to learn something and transmit something about their surroundings, about people's daily lives, their cares, fears, problems and joys.

(quoted in Daly 1986: 47)

The distinction between the two aesthetics concerns the presence of the dancer's body on stage. Either one works with the body as a formal element, to be moved and manipulated through various techniques; or with a body that is the subjective presence of the individual, expressing one's involvement in society through cultural and acculturated images and attitudes.

The critics involved in the discussion succinctly elucidate this point of divergence. Nancy Goldner of *The Philadelphia Inquirer* summarizes the American perspective:

Very generally speaking, I think that the chief characteristic of American dance is that choreographers are interested in movement values. Every gesture and every step has an inherent validity, beauty, and expressiveness. It's all there, all you have to do is use it. These American ideas come from two men in the warring camps of ballet and modern dance: George Balanchine and Merce Cunningham … I think younger choreographers – and some of them aren't so young anymore – have always used the idea, first, that movement is interesting in itself. That we dance so that we can express something but first of all we dance so we can move. The idea is to move – how are you going to move,

how many interesting ways can you do it. The second idea is that movements have in themselves an expressive quality.

(quoted in Daly 1986: 48–49)

In this scenario, it is the movement which is expressive, and the human body is a tool to elicit that movement. Jochen Schmidt calls on another tradition of American dance to counter this idea and hold up tanztheater as an example of dance where the human body as subject is expressive:

> I think there have been two lines in American modern dance: One is more realistic – Martha Graham, Doris Humphrey, José Limón and Anna Sokolow. But it was lost after Graham. I see a lot of younger American choreographers now doing things which classical ballet can do better. They are always trying to become brilliant and fast. I ask: Why don't they do ballet? For me, some of those dancers and choreographers are like hamsters. These little beasts in a wheel go around and around but always remain in the same spot.

(quoted in Daly 1986: 49)

The American critical response to the German dances ranged from revelatory and appreciative, to bemused, baffled, and downright angry. Sparks often arose from the friction of trying to force a subjective consideration of the body in German dance through the objective, formalist critical mind-set of American dance. Deborah Jowitt recognized the distinction between the two approaches to dance, but could not see these two perspectives merging into any kind of change in American dance practice. She said:

> I can't imagine American choreographers wishing to imitate "Tanztheater," no matter how much they are impressed by the work. It may be instructive to see that extremes of emotion can be dealt with on stage in innovative ways, but I think that American dancers still have faith in the expressive powers of dancing and form.

("What the Critics Say" 1986: 81)

In this case "dancing" is considered as the formal expression of movement through a developed technique, or, as Nancy Goldner characterizes it: "American dance is about moving bodies – dance for dance's sake, so to speak, and let the emotional chips fall where they

may" ("What the Critics Say" 1986: 81). The purity of formal values was never quite so marked as this simple division of aesthetics would imply, but nonetheless the influence of Bausch's work, and its far-ranging impact on European work since then, has opened up new possibilities in American modern dance. And while Bausch's work pushed open doors in the dance world (sometimes with some reluctance from the entrenched practitioners), theater artists were quick to embrace her large-scale imagistic works and claim their dream-like narrative structures as a continuation of theatrical experiments dating back to the turn of the last century. Despite American reluctance to fully accept the work at this point, Bausch's reputation had been made, and her place in European dance solidified.

RESIDENCY PIECES AS AN EXPANSION OF FORM 1986–98

Bausch has taken advantage of her increasing reputation to establish residency periods in different cities to explore new ideas and to use those as the basis for new work. This process started with a residency in Rome, where the company developed *Viktor* (1986). They explore the city and come back to rehearsals with their impressions. The company returns to Wuppertal for the arduous process of sifting through their reactions and developing the shape of the work, and the final piece premieres at their home opera house before returning to the city that inspired it for a further run. Although there were other types of pieces generated during this period (including a break to create a film, *Die Klage der Kaiserin* (*The Plaint of the Empress*, 1989)), the process increasingly becomes Bausch's preferred way of working. She creates pieces based on residencies in Palermo (*Palermo, Palermo*, 1989), Madrid (*Tanzabend II*, 1991), Vienna (*Ein Trauerspiel*, 1994), the American West (*Nur Du*, 1996, created primarily out of the company's residency in Los Angeles, but also with brief visits to San Francisco and Austin, Texas), Hong Kong (*Der Fensterputzer*, 1997), Lisbon (*Masurca Fogo*, 1998), and so on.

In these residency pieces, which continue to the present, Bausch is able to expand on her creative process of asking questions of the dancers and deriving material from their lives and past. She uses her company's response to place to uncover something more than simply a tourist's portrait of the city. She continually asks what makes the

people who they are? What gives the city its vibrancy and character? And that comes more out of the way people inhabit their lives than any of the particular details of the city itself. The goal is to find something more universal underlying the expressive possibilities uncovered in any given culture.

I was able to see some of this process in action when Bausch came to America to create what would become *Nur Du*. The company trained in the mornings at UCLA dance center, and rehearsed in the afternoons. They spent evenings exploring Los Angeles, visiting everything from a boxing gym to a UCLA basketball practice. They went on a whale-watching trip and bowling at Hollywood Bowl. They even saw popular 1970s television personality Florence Henderson receive her star on the Hollywood "Walk of Fame." Over fifty sites and events in all were visited. Bausch was interested in a variety of events, but was particularly drawn to situations where people move. She and her company all still do come from a dance background, and are keenly attuned to the way people express themselves in movement. The company had hoped to wander the streets and mingle with the people,

Figure 1.4 *Der Fensterputzer* (1997). Photo by Bettina Stöß

but the residents, spending most of their time in the world trapped in their cars, were not so easily observable.

After their stay, Rainer Behr, one of the members of the company, commented:

> Los Angeles seemed very poor to me, although not in a material but in a spiritual sense. So full of illusions … These opinions, these mindsets, these lives – to be honest, it really blew me away. Right there, in your face, the situation of all those who can't make it, who can't function … There, they've got the freedom to really live out their dumb things, their lost ideals. Everything is lived out, without limits.
>
> (quoted in "Thoughts on the Creation of *Nur Du* and Bausch's World" 1996: 30)

When asked how this wealth of experience would find its way into a dance, Bausch responded:

> I am looking for something I felt, or touched, or saw, or somebody I met. It could be something very simple – what happens because of the people who are there and how they interact. I would like to see, to learn, to meet, and then see what happens.
>
> (quoted in Breslauer 1996: 3)

The piece itself is a series of disconnected moments, epitomized for me by one simple image of presentation. Andrei Berezine enters with a rocking chair. He calls for Jan, and looks around, but Jan is not to be found. He sits in the rocker and lights a cigarette, and then, blowing smoke and looking supremely comfortable, he says: "Help." His tone is playfully facetious. He continues, "If something happens to you, call 911. After, do something, jump, scream. When they come they can see you." As opposed to many images from prior Bausch works that deliberately expose some element of the performers, all of these moments are performed as if there is a need to be seen in order to exist, that only in calling attention to yourself do you become yourself.

When asked how she thinks the American audience will respond to the work, Bausch explains:

> what I try is to find the pictures, or the images that can best express the feelings I want to convey. And you have to find your own way to show these

things. I am not telling a story in a normal way. Each person in the audience is part of the piece in a way; you bring your own experience, your own fantasy, your own feeling in response to what you see. There is something happening inside. You only understand if you let that happen, it's not something you can do with your intellect. So everybody, according to their experience, has a different feeling, a different impression.

(quoted in Meisner 1992: 15)

Each moment in *Nur Du* has individual value, but the real strength of the piece comes in accretion. We are left with a feeling of isolation and desperate showcasing, of arrogance and resiliency, and a surface sheen that is hardened and shined to mirror-like quality, but that does not permit entry into any interior world (actual mirrors, from hand-held compacts, to full-length mirrors, appear frequently in the piece). Although some of the California critics were reluctant to see this as a portrayal of the American West, for me the overall effect transcends specific references to address deeper connections that are particularly American. And, as usual in Bausch's pieces, there was room to derive from the evening whatever you were willing to put into it. If you came looking for some entertaining moments, they were there to be had, and if you invested more of your own place in the world, you might find a way to approach the surface values we all confront in our daily lives.

Throughout this period, Bausch is still working within the same basic conceptual frame she established in that defining period described above. The ground of the work is a physical entrance into inner dimensions through highly crafted sequences of evocative images. The pieces are built like dreams, with seemingly unrelated moments actually showing an internal consistency of underlying intent. The motivating impulse for the work shifts during this period, however. It started as the lives of her dancers themselves, but now moves toward a kind of cultural anthropology. Bausch asks how we perform ourselves, and shows the results of her and her company's exploration, carefully crafted into cubist portraits that present multiple perspectives that all adhere to an inner logic. If anything, the work during this period is more refined, settling into a groove as both Bausch and the company (and the audience) become accustomed to this type of work. But I find the work losing some of the vitality of that early creative period. It feels to me to be one step removed from the immediacy of

those early works, and the step back gives the audience a bit more room for comfort.

RETURNING TO DANCE, 1999–

Nur Du is punctuated by several solos done in more of a conventional movement-based dance idiom. The men in particular shine through these isolated moments, all of which incorporate a certain degree of dramatic gesture pushed toward full body swoops and collapses to the floor. The piece ends with one final solo, done by Dominique Mercy, a brilliant dancer who continues to amaze even as he approaches sixty. He hurls his graceful body into the space and flails his arms with abandon. This final dance appears to be a dance of death, where we witness the last gasps of a dying bird, like the death of the swan in *Swan Lake*, done double time. I left feeling that after all the surface gloss we have been shown, and the many humorous moments, we are left with the fragility of one individual confronting death. A solitary man, out of context, going through his final attempts to hold on to life.

Bausch had included more movement-based prompts in the rehearsal period for this piece. The company is in transition, as well. Some of the old stalwarts have moved on, and a new crop of younger dancers takes their place. Bausch's reputation ensures that she is able to recruit the best the dance world has to offer. The company had always been international, but by this point it is pointedly so, with a few representatives from every continent. Bausch had said that she needed to leave dance aside for a time in the 1980s, and here now in the mid-1990s, she begins to re-approach ideas of movement. There had always been moments of movement in the work, but the combination of the changing composition of the company and Bausch's own comfort in her style allow those moments to become more prominent. But even as she re-establishes a base in more conventional movement phrases, the process remains that probing exploration of self and place.

In the early work, many of the company members were ready to move outside the boundaries that dance created. The newer company members don't feel the same restrictions through dance, in part because of Bausch's influence in opening up possibility in the first place, and so are ready to express their ideas and emotions through movement. Bausch takes what the company offers and responds to

what they need and what the piece demands. In no other company is the work such a reflection of individual company members. Seeing successive pieces, you come to know the different dancers and recognize their contributions to the work, and this transition in the work can be mapped on the changing composition of the company. I hadn't realized, for instance, quite how important Jan Minarik's influence had been until he retired. He still works with the company as a consultant, but his forceful presence is no longer felt on stage. Minarik had been uncompromising in his push of the boundaries of expression to uncover the subtlety of character, often exposing his own fragile vulnerability in the process. Other dancers fill in for the older pieces in repertoire, and are able to bring out this reverberant quality of performance, but the new pieces are constructed along different lines.

We first start to see that transition with *Nur Du*, and its return to dance. But that piece is still very much built on the imagistic ground of the earlier work, and many of the older company members still hold considerable sway, even as the new recruits start to find their voice. *Masurca Fogo* (1998) is the most buoyantly gleeful mix of the old and the new. There is still a mixture of imagistic structures and more movement-centered passages, but whether because of the influence of the new company members, or the passion of Lisbon on which the piece is based, there is a youthful energy and sensuality to the piece that points us in a new direction.

The next several pieces Bausch has done have still been based on residencies in various cities, with a similar anthropological approach, but there is a different feeling to the work. Part of it is the increase of more traditional dance-centered movement sequences. More apparent, however, is the ease with which the company moves through the work. The early work had a defiant quality, as if we were witness to an event, and not always a willing witness, as we were being shown how we are in the world and how we treat each other. The results were not always comfortable, but always revelatory. Now, I enjoy the pieces and marvel at the craftsmanship in both construction and performance, but I no longer feel my life is being ripped from my own protective cloak, laid bare and strewn across the stage.

Despite the lasting impact of Bausch's incorporation of theatrical presentational influences into a dance-centered dramaturgical structure and visceral physical presence, her more recent work returns to

Figure 1.5 Dominique Mercy in *Ten Chi* (2004). Photo by Bettina Stöß

dance, but now having passed through the transformative atmosphere of theatrical consciousness and carrying the weight of a new way of approaching an audience and creating work in a radicalized world. The ground-breaking expansion of form came from a desire within her and her company to find a new means of expression, one that captured the immediacy of their concerns. They explored new ways of being on stage, and subsequently opened the door for other choreographers and theater artists to explore a new means of representation, one that accounts for and utilizes the real presence of the performer's body, without attempting to push his or her body through an objective technique, and without trying to make his or her body stand for something else in the presentation of character within a dramatic story.

Once that door had been opened, Bausch and her company set about charting the limits of the world on the other side. They continue to respond more to their own needs – as performers, as people – rather than to the dictates of a theatrical or dance community, or to an audience that might want to see more of the same. Their reputation gives them the freedom to continually ask that question from which Bausch started: "What moves you?" The answers

Figure 1.6 *Nefes* (2003). Photo by Bettina Stöß

come in the shape of new pieces, responding to new residencies, and to an increasingly younger core of dancers and an aging Bausch. The tensions of placement in a hostile world become the satisfied but slightly rueful look back at the struggles of youth. And there is a comfort in the work, in having achieved a place from which to say that which before was not possible to be said. Bausch created the possibility to say it.

BAUSCH'S WORK AND CONTEMPORARY THEATER

Even as Bausch returns to a more movement-based dance idiom, her impact on theater continues to grow. The initial impulse for the work came out of that fervent reimagining of theatrical potential under way during Bausch's formative years. Experimental theater in the 1960s, often working from the prophetic ideas of theatrical rebel Antonin Artaud, initiated a process of redefining subjectivity and visceral presence on stage. It became possible, through the experiments of a variety of theater artists, to create a world *of* the stage rather than a world *on* the stage, and the human relation of the performer shifted from one absorbed in character to one as elemental and actual. It is this kind of energy from which Bausch draws, and in which she finds herself enmeshed during her time in New York in the 1960s and as she begins her own work in Germany in the 1970s.

The theater world of Bausch's educational years was one of increasing physicality and immediacy, a natural bridge from her dance background and growing frustration with formalist tendencies in dance. The importance of recognizing Bausch's placement within this theatrical continuum lies in the energy from which she drew. She found ways to engage that energy within her own means, and, I think, can easily be placed alongside other major contributors to theater practice of the late twentieth century. Her grand schemes and epic works are often placed alongside similarly grand work by theatrical legends like Peter Brook (b.1925) or Ariane Mnouchkine (b.1939).

In addition to Bausch's connection to theatrical pioneers like Artaud and Grotowski, more recently Bausch's work has been compared to that of a wide range of theater artists and styles. In her use of visual metaphor, critics have seen parallels between her work and the precise visual language employed by Robert Wilson (b.1941). Her working

environment has been linked to the intellectual playing spaces developed by Richard Foreman (b.1937) with his Ontological Hysteric Theater. Foreman describes his working space as "an environment for the text to explore, a gymnasium for a psychic, spiritual and physical workout" (Foreman, 1995: 69), and absent the concentration on text, that description would certainly be apt for the environment Bausch creates. The way her pieces are brought together through exploration in rehearsal has been placed alongside similar work by the New York-based Wooster Group, and later work by Ann Bogart (b.1951) and SITI Company's use of "Viewpoints" as a way to import principles of dance construction to theatrical development. Bausch's particular developmental approach and move toward theater through physicality has been compared to the movement and sound operas of Meredith Monk (b.1942) as well.

What all of these artists and styles of performance share more than any governing aesthetic is simply the search for new forms of expression outside of conventional dramatic structure. The work of most of these artists, including that of Bausch, has been labeled as performance art at some point in their careers, even as the relatively recently coined term retroactively claimed the Futurists, Dada, and much other experimental theater practice of the twentieth century. In many ways, performance art, as a term, is useful to describe those events that fall outside the accepted ground of what theater or dance can be at that time. It is a process of growth, constantly making itself obsolete as performances and styles are accepted into the now expanded field of what theater or dance can mean. It is by definition the leading edge of performance practice. Bausch's work has extended the boundaries of what dance and theater are, and in the process blurred the boundaries between both.

BAUSCH'S INFLUENCE

Bausch's influence has worked along (at least) two different lines. First, her work expands the palette of formal resources performing artists can use. Bausch opens the door to new creative process which allows choreographers, directors, and creators of new works to reach toward the center of an idea, a play, or a creative construct and articulate that heart through a variety of means. Second, Bausch's work opens possibility. What you once may have viewed as a boundary – between theater

and dance, text and movement, character and performer, and so on — is shown to be a limiting structure that can be pushed aside, and dozens of individual artists and creators have taken on that challenge.

What Bausch appears to do with such ease in creating these fluid, dream-like pieces that explode the boundaries of the stage, is not so simple to accomplish in practice. In Bausch's oeuvre, the pieces come from months of painstaking creative work, editing, orchestrating, and rebuilding. Those who might wish to walk through the door of possibility Bausch provides must confront a difficult process. Nonetheless, despite the spate of poor imitations of Bausch that have appeared on stages around the world, there have also been several who have used the tools and freedom they inherit from Bausch in combination with the vast variety of their own talents to create challenging and dynamic work.

In her home country, other German artists have expanded on the ground that Bausch established. The older generation of artists who worked alongside Bausch in the years when tanztheater was developed still hold significant influence, while many among the newer generation create compelling work. None has received more attention than Sasha Waltz (b.1963). After studying in Amsterdam and America, Waltz created a number of viscerally demanding pieces for which she credits Bausch's work as a direct influence. In 2000, she was asked to be an Artistic Associate at the Schaubühne in Berlin where she continues to work creating dynamic pieces alongside director Thomas Ostermeier's (b.1968) reimagining of theatrical possibility. In Switzerland, Joachim Schlömer (b.1962) (another product of the Folkwang School) has worked as the head of Tanztheater Basel since the mid-1980s. Anne Teresa de Keersmaeker (b.1960) and her company Rosas lead what has been dubbed the Belgian dance-theater boom, with works that range from stunning formal expressions (*Fase* (1982), *Rosas Danst Rosas* (1983), and the more recent *Small Hands (out of the lie of no)* (2001)) to pieces that fuse theatrical elements with rigorous physical expression (*Elena's Aria* (1984), *Stella* (1990) and *(but if a look should) April me* (2002) among others) and some newer works that explore text: *Quartett* (1999, text by Heiner Mueller) and *I said I* (1999, text by Peter Handke). She also explicitly cites Bausch as an influence in her construction of new works. She is followed by a group of artists exploding the boundaries between dance and theater: Wim Vandekeybus (b.1963) and Ultima Vez, Meg Stuart (b.1965) and Damaged Goods, NeedCompany, Alain Platel (b.1959),

and so on, all of whom list Bausch as a primary influence. Bausch's work has also opened new possibilities in dance around the globe, from France to Israel, India to South America.

England is in the midst of a new wave of physical theater, while the dance scene also moves to expand boundaries. While the seminal work of theater groups like Theatre de Complicité or Forced Entertainment or the visceral dance of DV8 can't be traced directly back to Bausch's influence, the move toward a direct confrontation of physicality in space and time and away from a more text-based dramaturgy certainly comes from an evocative atmosphere Bausch's work significantly impacted (and many company members in all of those groups count themselves amongst Bausch's many fans). The impact is seen not always in new physicality, but in the developmental process and use of dance-construction principles to interweave theatrical images.

American dance has clearly moved beyond the formal considerations cited in the 1980s, if it wasn't already moving in new directions even at that point. Choreographers work to find ways to incorporate the broader impact of theatrical presentation while maintaining a base in physical expression, often amidst increasingly constrained (financial) resources. New theater companies have added to the challenge of text-based work and sought new possibilities of construction. Downtown performance festivals in New York are peppered with groups exploring a physical base of development, coming out of both Bausch's influence and the increasing importance of the Viewpoints as a means of exploring new performance work. (Created by Mary Overlie from roots in expressionist dance practice and further developed by Anne Bogart and SITI Company, Viewpoints open up a performer's awareness in time and space.) All these groups share a response to the open dramaturgical structure of which Bausch provides the foremost example. Bausch's work has changed the ground of presentation, and offered a new way in for dance and theater practitioners across the spectrum of performance.

Bausch's initial aims in her choreography were echoes of her German expressionist roots: to explore the potential of the stage and lay bare the depth of human emotion. One of Bausch's greatest achievements in the development of tanztheater has been to draw on the power of those essential elements of the stage and of presentation. Bausch refuses to take anything for granted, always asking both what it means and what it does simply to walk out on stage and be looked at, and look back. In so doing, she utilizes stage elements for what

they are, rather than what they pretend to be, and concentrates her attention on the performers themselves, and what they can offer in rehearsal. She strips away the ornate exterior to uncover people.

The combination of that concentration on the subjective presence of her performers, who bring their own histories, ideas, knowledge, and experience to bear on each performed moment, and the very questioning of that arena of display in theater and dance leads to a form of presentation that consciously incorporates vast histories of social engagement and performance practice. Each moment is built on the same ground through which we perceive it, never innocently, but always in light of our own experience and history, expectations and awareness of the past. The present moment is built on a past that runs deep, and allows that moment to breathe its small gulp of air before it too becomes one more piece necessary for the construction of the next present.

All that is a longer way of saying that Bausch does not let us off easily. The moments she creates are the glistening tips of very large icebergs that bring with them the weight of intricate social and historical layering. Each moment can be appreciated for the glistening portion above the surface, but an awareness of the depth and intricacy of the precedents that keep that moment afloat can add a new level of understanding. We see Bausch's pieces both from our own developed present, and within the context of the performed history they embody. Tanztheater develops out of the multiplicity of those influences, rather than as a further development of a specific performance practice. Bausch's own life and creative development provide a model for the energies that lead to the essential difference that the development of tanztheater contains. She carries that history with her, and the work is a constant reflection of it.

WHAT IS SAID

BAUSCH ON BAUSCH

Whenever I mention to people in the performing arts that I am researching and writing about Pina Bausch, the first question they ask is how she does what she does. It's hard enough to describe precisely what it is that she does, but theater and dance artists can see it; they see something different in her works, something provocative that subtly changes the ground of performance practice. Still, the question lingers, "How does she do that?"

Many innovative artists spend years developing a method, a system of working, and often refine that process by writing about it throughout their lives. The attempt to get your ideas down on paper forces you to come to concrete terms, and perhaps come up with useful resources for others to draw on as they create their own ways of working.

Pina Bausch assiduously avoids talking about her pieces, let alone writing anything down. Even when she was young, she turned to dance to avoid speaking. "I loved to dance because I was scared to speak. When I was moving, I could feel" (quoted in Lawson 2000: 18). That early fear may echo her concern that speaking about her performances too much pins them down and robs them of the open interpretation she strives for. She wants an audience to bring their own ideas, histories, and connections to the pieces.

The expression happens on stage, and the work to uncover that expression happens in the rehearsal hall. Words merely become an inconvenient and poor substitute for the immediacy of expression that can take place through the dynamics of performance. In trying to explain how she began her work, she recently said:

> I wanted to express something that I couldn't express with words at all. Something I have to say urgently, but not verbally. These are feelings, or questions, I never have an answer. I am dealing with something that we all sense, that occupies all of us in a similar language. I am the audience as well. And when I see, I feel something. I can only come from my own instinct. When I trust my feeling, I believe it's not only mine. I share it with others.
>
> (Bausch, 2004a, my translation: 9)

That sharing takes place in live performance, where she would like the piece to speak for itself. As she explained during what was supposed to be a lecture series at Stanford, "I don't have many words because what I have to say I try to express through my work on stage" (quoted in Manuel 1999: n.p.). She proceeded to have her dancers perform small sections of the piece as her form of lecture. One of her favorite anecdotes is about when, after playing a piano piece he had composed, someone asked Beethoven what he meant by the piece. He simply turned back to the piano and played it again. She says the same thing about her own performances. "When we have danced the *Sacre*, we have nothing more to say about it. We have said it in our dance. *Sacre*, as a work, just is!" (Bausch 1985: 19)

But Bausch does speak, despite her reticence, and speak eloquently about the struggle to create, refining a way of working, and the importance of people in her process, in all their sad and vulnerable beauty. Even in describing Bausch's reluctance to speak, I have tried to use her own words to bring out the feeling of her opinions. Clearly, live experience is the best way to come to an understanding of her work, both as individual pieces and as an oeuvre, but I hope there is something to be gained through Bausch's words about the pieces, and particularly about her process; that persistent question of how she does what she does.

The model for this series of books is to provide a section outlining the performance practitioner's written works. With no books, essays,

or even lectures to draw on, analyzing Bausch's own thoughts can be difficult, but she has given numerous interviews, in German and English, where she articulates an intricate process of developing her work. I have tried to let Bausch speak throughout this chapter, including a previously unpublished interview with Ruth Berghaus transcribed from an open forum discussion in Berlin in 1987. Bausch's own words construct the fabric of her approach to her work, and help us to see its necessity and impact.

DEFINING PROCESS

In early interviews, Bausch often received questions about how she builds her pieces. You can almost hear interviewers longing for a method statement, hoping Bausch will reply with a definitive declaration about her treatment of the body in space and time, as many modern dance pioneers had before her.

The closest approximation to a method Bausch divulges is asking questions. Describing the process that developed during that pivotal period of redefinition during work on *Bluebeard* and then with actors and dancers on *Macbeth*, she says:

> I went into retreat with four dancers in Jan Minarik's little studio and we started work – with very few people. And then the others began to come back of their own accord – but only if they wanted to; I didn't want anyone who wasn't prepared to work. During this process I began to ask questions, to formulate my own questions within the circle – which was in itself a self-questioning for me and for the others as well. I could only dare to do this within a small circle. The method became clearly apparent during the work in Bochum [on the *Macbeth* project]. There we had four dancers, four actors and a singer – the dancers didn't dance, the actors didn't act and the singer didn't sing. I'd made up my mind to use *Macbeth* as a basis for the work. It was a way of seeing how we could work things out together – I couldn't just turn up with a complete movement sequence. That was a significant piece for the invention of this working method.
>
> (Bausch 1995: 36)

Bausch began to uncover a working method during this time, and she has refined that process throughout the past thirty years, but the struggle to create still exists. Confronting the empty stage at the

beginning of rehearsals is always difficult, and devising a way to approach the work doesn't necessarily make things easier, nor does all of the praise she has received move her past the feelings of doubt which always plague her in beginning a new piece.

> Nothing helps me. Not what I have already done. It is done. Each time, you are a beginner. I want to give up, actually, but I don't … it's complicated. It all takes so much strength. I'm so fragile. It's emotional. I get little sleep, you try to sleep, but you can't. I'm thinking too much. It's like my head is in the way. It seems simple, but I make it so complicated. It gets worse when I am coming out of a work. There comes a point when I think "This is the last time. I am never going to do this again." And afterwards, you think "I should not stop now. I should right away do a new piece." I go to all the extremes, deep down. It's so terrible, horrible, you go down, down, down, but you can't give up, because the dancers are always there and expect you to do something.
>
> (quoted in Lawson 2000: 19)

What most choreographers have to hang on to in the midst of the downward spiral in the face of creative possibility is a means of creating movement. If you get to that point of being overwhelmed, you can always go back to the basics, create movement patterns, and let that drive you forward. Interviewers push at Bausch to define her means of creating movement, to articulate a "Bausch technique."

Bausch doesn't appear to understand the question, or at least shows very little interest in it. What does interest her, and what she comes back to time and again, are people. Beyond her career-defining statement "I'm not so interested in how they move as in what moves them" (quoted in Schmidt 1984: 15–16), early interviews are full of statements about the importance of people and the difficulties of dealing with all of their personality quirks, vulnerabilities, and needs. And yet this is exactly what the process is built on. Bausch's early work, and the fleeting snippets of description she allows in describing it, all emphasize the necessity of group process and individual input into the work. The answer to the question "How do I do what she does?" – which I have also asked myself time and again as I try to incorporate some of those methods into my own performance work – increasingly comes down to the importance of working collaboratively with a group of people with whom you build a relationship of mutually shared expression, exposure, and trust.

Performance qualities are less important than what each individual brings to the process, and objective qualities are irrelevant. Early on, she says, "I pick my dancers as people. I don't pick them for nice bodies, for having the same height, or things like that. I look for the person ... the personality" (Bausch 1985: 14). Each dancer's personality shines through in performance, more than simply in giving the movement a particular energy, but in the very makeup of the pieces themselves, and it is that personal material that brings out the underlying feelings of the piece. "Each of the dancers is, in a different way, important. Each has his own dances and his own way of dancing. It's not just doing choreography, but it's being aware of the feelings we all have and how we experience that. It's better just to see it" (quoted in Manuel 1999: n.p.).

Relying on what each individual performer brings to the process of creating a piece gives the work its depth and universality, but it also means coping with the vagaries of people's reactions and behavior: "I deal with human beings and all their complications, frustrations. They have private problems, jealousies. There are many different individuals in my company, and they all want to be loved very much and they are very sensitive. And each day you have to keep it alive, to explore and find a harmony. Every day it is a discovery" (Bausch 1999: 10C) But that doesn't mean she expects her dancers to simply open their lives and hearts to her. "I'm scared of people who do like this." She gestures a ripping out of her heart. "I like people who are difficult to open. Otherwise there's nothing special" (quoted in Mackrell 1999: C1).

Bausch emphasizes the importance of tenderness and respect in rehearsal, for creating an environment where people can open up, and for the kindness it takes to allow a piece to come into shape. She is just as involved in the delicate personal construction, and the dancers come to respect that as well. Working through a developed technique may provide a means to get the process moving, but it also often provides a screen, a structure to hide behind rather than deal with the raw vulnerability of wrestling with the questions she poses. Bausch explains the way people work in developing her pieces:

I don't have a technique. If I knew a better way to do my pieces, I would take it. It's not a principle. It is important that the base is confidential, that it comes out of a sense of what the dancers offer in confidence. I ask so many questions during the work, but I can't think of a single one at the moment. The dancers

need to have faith to answer what they feel – within the group, in front of everybody. And they need to have the faith that I will do something with it, but with respect, so that I have the freedom to ask them anything. Everybody has the same chances of contributing to the piece, suddenly one person becomes more important, in another piece it's someone else. And when someone does something stupid, we all laugh. We laugh a lot anyway. In the end it's about finding the right things. There is also the time when the dancers need to have a lot of patience with me when I am trying to do something with these extracts. Then I am penetrating and persnickety and I do the most stupid things. I'll try anything possible, but I still may not find how it should work. Suddenly, I don't believe in what I was thinking or what I had planned, I only believe what I have seen. It's so simple. Sometimes I think I'm asking the wrong questions all the time. Somehow, I know where it wants to go. I can't exactly name it, but when you find a form for it, you know it belongs.

(Bausch, 2004a, my translation: 5–6)

Bausch insists that all she does is ask questions, and watch. Of course there is a lot to even those seemingly simple activities, but the added dimension is not what she asks, but who she is asking. Her early work, and especially the move from the more dance-centered pieces to the developmental process based pieces starting with *Bluebeard*, echoes her efforts to distill a cohesive group around her and begin to define a collective expressive palette.

Bausch is the leader, but the efforts of the entire company are what make the pieces function. Bausch's company taps into that collective energy, both providing a model for and echoing any number of companies working in this way, most from a theatrical perspective, from Theatre de Complicité to the Wooster Group, Forced Entertainment to SITI Company. The group ideology and developmental process become driving forces and a vortex that draws company members in. As one of Bausch's dancers said:

You know, I love her and I hate her. She is remarkable, but she can drive you so hard. Sometimes she doesn't seem to care that you are only human, that you can do only so much. At other times, she has the most concern you can imagine. I went away, finally, but I had to come back. Nowhere else can I have this experience as a dancer.

(quoted in Bausch 1985: 17)

HOW WE GET THERE

Once Bausch has filled the room with a diverse group of performers, all committed to the process of creation, the question of "What now?" still hangs in the air. Without a technique, and without a script to follow and respond to, how does the work in rehearsals proceed? This is where Bausch's comments can feel particularly elliptic. She talks about asking questions, but how does that simple act work its way into a piece? What interviews reveal as the coalescing influence is patience, and the temerity to keep pushing at an idea until connections begin to emerge. That process is the fundamental question at the heart of Bausch's discussion led by Ruth Berghaus in Berlin in 1987. She had described this process in previous interviews, but here she opens up the stages of development in more detail.

INTERVIEW WITH RUTH BERGHAUS, BERLIN, MAY 29, 1987 (TRANSLATED BY ELLEN CREMER AND ROYD CLIMENHAGA, AND EDITED BY ROYD CLIMENHAGA)

Ruth: In the wonderful performances we saw, the various elements of the production all come together and begin to impact each other. How do you develop this unusual expressive palette for dance?

Pina: The working process – how we put a piece together – has of course changed a lot. In the beginning I planned every move, very specifically. Out of fear. I wanted to make it good, and so I planned everything in advance – he is doing this, she is doing that – and then the costumes, the stage design, etc. Everything in its place. And while I was working I would suddenly see things that just happened and that interested me, and so the question came up: Do I follow my plan or do I follow what I just saw? I always followed what was new, never my plan. I always thought, this other idea, that I saw right there, might be more important, even though I had no idea where it was leading. At one point I had the courage not to make a plan at all. When I make a piece now, it is only out of what is present at the time. I try to feel what I feel.

I am the audience. Me alone. There is nobody else. I don't even know who will come to the theater – people I don't know anything about. For whom should I make this piece? I can only start from myself. I am sitting there and I am the audience, and I feel, and I laugh, and I am afraid or sad or whatever happens to me. I can only offer ideas and suggest, but I am the thermometer.

Also, when we begin we have no idea what we are going to do with the space, no set, no music, nothing else except us and how we respond in the moment. Only after a while when you notice where the piece is going can you ask: In what kind of space could or should something like this happen? Actually, it is the same with the music we choose. We play with things and then suddenly they are there where we think they need to be. There is something so specific about music. When you play through a scene with ten different musical choices, it's a different story each time. Sometimes I have music that I would like to use, but I can't because it doesn't fit into the piece. Sometimes, five years later, this music comes back into a piece where it fits. Matthias Burkert takes care of that. He asks me what I think might fit and then we look for it and sometimes we don't find anything for a long time. It's similar with the costumes. We get this huge pile of stuff (mostly second hand) and we try things. Someone tries this, someone else that. But the performers don't bring their own clothes, it is more organized than that. Marion Cito is in charge of that, and she has been my assistant since 1980.

Ruth: Where does the theme of an evening come from?

Pina: From a feeling from within. What I said before, I try to feel what I feel in the moment, and out of that I find questions for my dancers. All the questions come from me. After class we meet and I ask a question. We all think about it. The questions are very simple, everybody can give an answer or say something about it. We write it down or keep it in mind. Then there are more ideas that add to it and through what I see there are more new threads, new ideas. All of this material, in this initial stage, is not the piece. But there are different little things that come out of that and they have something to do with what I am actually looking for, but which has no clear image or form yet. So, there is no theme – except what presents itself. Ultimately, I'm always dealing with the same thing.

Audience: It seems that fear is a major theme in your work. Are you in a state of fear when you work?

Pina: You always look forward to starting a new piece because everything is so open. But somehow I am (I don't know how it is for others), but I am afraid, or I have to confront different fears. There is the fear that you won't be able to do what you want to, and the fear of not being able to deal with other people. But that is a different chapter.

I am not someone who just says nice things in rehearsal. I can't do that at all. Usually, I say very little, terribly little. And when you don't understand each other it becomes complicated. You become insecure and there are these things happening that you can't even talk about. You get stuck in these moments instead of progressing into the piece.

And when I finish a process, when I say I can't continue searching, when I begin to put things outside of myself more firmly, it becomes even more diffi-cult. I'm always afraid to stop. I would like to keep pushing at it. But this pro-cess can't go on forever because we have to be finished, we have a deadline – opening night.

Audience: How does the text come together?

Pina: The texts come from the same process. For example, in the piece you saw yesterday [*1980 – A Piece by Pina Bausch*], the performers describe the country they come from in three words. That simply came out of a question in rehearsal about identity, how are you who you are? Sometimes it works like that, but sometimes we just have to keep looking because our first idea didn't fit. Or sometimes what people say has changed after a while in performance, or we change things because in Italy or France certain words may not be familiar. But I think that moment of description would work anywhere.

Audience: Do individual performers find particular words or phrases – and do those words stay the same no matter who may take on that role?

Pina: It depends on how the moment works. Usually what someone does connects with their personality. But it can also happen that everybody does what one person has created, or we can play around with it and when it doesn't fit with one character anymore, we give it to someone else. But most of the time the things you see or hear are performed by the people who came up with then. What you see in performance is only a small percentage of the actual material we develop, however. I look at the material during rehearsal and I let go of about half of it immediately. I push at and question the other half again. And then we repeat it, not in an order, but sometimes this, then that. Everyone should remember it all. That works pretty well.

After a while, I start to see the material more cohesively, because everyone can just do it and we don't need to wait in between things so much to think and remember. The material becomes smaller, even though it is still way too much. What I don't need at all is gone already. Then I say: Let's try to combine this and that, and let's see. Maybe I find something small that means a lot more to me. Then I'll find a different entry point. I never start from the very beginning. I don't work from the beginning to the end, but with small parts that slowly become larger, and so the piece slowly comes together and expands. And let's say I have ten parts that have already become large sections, and lots of single things. Only then can I start thinking of how I want the piece to begin. Only then. This has always been my method. But that doesn't mean anything, there are so many ways to do things. Unfortunately, I can't do it

differently. I am extremely thorough. It is terrible because I turn everything around and I make it more difficult for myself. Terrible.

Audience: What were your impulses and motivations when you first started working. Did you want to find something different than classical ballet?

Pina: At one point I started doing something because I wanted to dance. I never thought I would create a complete piece or become a choreographer. I didn't feel challenged enough and I wanted to do something that I felt. There was time, there were people who wanted to join in. And so we did something. The only reason was: to dance. And that piece came into being like that. It was fun. And I must say I was never thinking it must be ballet or it shouldn't be ballet at all. I liked to move in this kind of way and when I set out to do something on my own it was in that particular form. It wasn't a sense of wanting to make something better or rejecting something else. When I came to Wuppertal, there was a ballet company. It was not about doing something completely different or to slowly do something differently, or looking for a smooth transition. It has never happened like that. I tried to do what I thought I had to do.

Ruth: When something new appears it is most often because it has to. The burden of creating something new, the difficulties, you only take that on if you have to.

Audience: Was there resistance in the beginning?

Pina: The opposite. I came to Wuppertal the very first time at the request of the director. He had the courage to say: Look, find a group, find people you want to work with. I didn't have the courage. I hadn't tried anything like that yet, I had only done very small pieces. I had no idea if I could do it or not. But he believed in me and kept asking until I said, "Yes, I will try." And that was a bold choice on his part, against the city, against many people. I think most of them didn't like the idea of my kind of work in the first place. It was mainly the director at that time, and later on others, who allowed me to work. It was difficult with the audience. I was lucky because none of the directors ever said: Can't you make things differently, or do something similar to what's already been done? No one has ever said that to me. I don't know how I would have reacted.

Audience: Are you able to let go of expectations and the pressure of the press and publicity in creating the work?

Pina: Yes. I have to. We always start at point zero. All of these expectations are stupid clichés.

Ruth: But you always run that risk in this profession.

Pina: Yes, always. One is always misunderstood. I can't avoid that. I felt angry about that quite often. But now it doesn't bother me anymore. Because I don't deal with it anymore. When you begin to deal with it you don't have time to work anymore. It's true, it eats you up otherwise.

Audience: How do you maintain the quality of your performances?

Pina: Through performing. When someone leaves it's very difficult to replace that person. The problem is, nothing is written down. No one has time to do that. We don't have anyone who is responsible for that. We have videos to keep things that would get lost otherwise, but we can only learn by performing, because it came into being through the group. So it only works if we hope that we stay together and don't forget it.

Audience: How do you choose the cast?

Pina: Usually, everyone participates. I only did two pieces where I wanted to work with fewer people. Otherwise there are as many people in the piece as we have in the company at that time. In *Sacre du Printemps* there were even more, some dancers from the Folkwang School joined us. If someone wasn't a part of a production it was only because that person had a specific scheduling conflict or needed a break. If that's the case, I suggest that they skip this piece, because I can't give anyone performances off.

Audience: Do you consider acting skills when you hire a dancer?

Pina: In an audition we do regular classical training and then everybody learns a phrase from *Sacre*, for example. Even there, I can already see a lot, but I don't see anything about how they might use language or any specific acting skills. That is always a surprise. I never just leave it at what I can see in their dancing. Of course I am hoping to find a good dancer, and sometimes I can only see afterwards those performance qualities that I choose more instinctively. Those qualities were why I said "yes, we'll give it a try."

And strangely enough, I've never gone wrong, even if everything seemed to go against my choice. Sometimes the group didn't understand why I hired someone. They couldn't see what I found so special about this person. Two years later, they could see it. That is always very difficult. I can only hope, I never know for sure.

But I am curious. I like them all and somehow I learn from all of them. Not in the sense of knowledge, but something else. Sometimes I realize that I have something similar in me and I didn't recognize it. I had always thought, this is who I am and suddenly I realize, here I have a little facet and here another one. Everyone has so many colors, you don't even know until you see them suddenly reflected in a new person. And I think we all learn through what we see. That is important.

For example, if someone is new and has been working in a group for a very long time, he will answer questions in the way he is used to. There are all these clichés, as you can imagine. It's not that easy to simply answer a question. You try to do it the best you can, but it doesn't always get at something

that is true for you. Sometimes it takes a long time before someone can get beyond all of these clichés and simply answer from themselves. I have noticed that new dancers in the group always go through this amazing frustration, and they become incredibly sad and distraught until suddenly something from deep down begins to come out. You can't force it, it just happens.

REPRESENTATION AS PROCESS, PROCESS AS REPRESENTATION

Bausch's approach to representation is essentially descriptive, but takes as its starting point the condition of our bodies in the revelation of experience. She probes the personal to find underlying behavior patterns which point toward the universal. Joys and fears, frustrations and confusions of everyday life are mined to find their kernel of hidden truth, and this truth is an active process of connection, different for each audience member.

Most of the members of the ensemble, past and present, come with substantial dance training, often in classical ballet technique. The initial audition process is centered on movement qualities, even if Bausch is looking beyond that movement to the person underneath. Some take to the new way of working more readily, and some struggle to shed preconceived notions about what dance should be. As Bausch says, "To understand what I am saying, you have to believe that dance is something other than technique. We forget where the movements come from. They are born from life. When you create a new work, the point of departure must be contemporary life – not existing forms of dance" (Bausch 1989: 91).

Even working from that statement, it is possible to imagine a movement-centered technique with an emphasis on personal expression. That is precisely what Mary Wigman worked toward throughout her career. The move from that expressionist dance structure to Bausch's defining work required a different base, one that redefined the possibilities of what could be dance. Bausch asks, "What is dance anyway? First of all, dance is not only a certain style, there are so many different styles, cultures, reasons to dance; we can't only call certain modern or ballet techniques dance, or say this is dance, this is not. For me, much more is dance than other people think of" (Bausch 1992: 16).

Figure 2.1 *Nelken* (1982). Photo by Bettina Stöß

What dance becomes for Bausch is a confrontation with behavior and bodily presentation, it is an organization of action that addresses life itself rather than an imitation created from the comfortable distance of an intermediary technique. Dance had always concerned itself with the possibilities of physical expression, but never before has that expression been extended to include the way in which we define our selves through our bodily relationship to cultural codes. The dancer's body on stage is freed from the rules of a developed technique to represent each individual's physical connection to a world of his or her own creation.

STRUCTURE

Bausch's early work with Tanztheater Wuppertal was built on more traditional principles of dance construction, and the rehearsal period mirrored that as dancers learned complicated series of movements handed down from the choreographer. *Rite of Spring* and the two Gluck operas *Iphigenie* and *Orpheus* had begun to open up possibilities of individual engagement, but were still primarily built on the model

of dance as a series of movements. As we saw in Chapter 1, *Bluebeard* provided the break for a new means of presentation, and it grew out of a new means of rehearsal and development. Company member Ruth Amarante explains, "I think it started with *Blaubart*. She started asking the company members questions, leaving it open as to how the person wanted to reply. You could answer in the form of movement, by talking, or by doing whatever you had in mind" (quoted in Fernandes 2001: 111). The questions begin to open up experience, and the work in rehearsals becomes the slow uncovering of the base operating principle of the idea or feeling in question. How do we experience love, loss, brutality, compassion, tenderness, and so on? Each performed moment in rehearsal becomes a possible avenue of further exploration.

The questions reveal the way in which the performers are contained through their experience, how they experience individual moments of connection. Amarante continues, "Many questions are about how it was in our countries, culturally specific questions; how was our childhood ... important people in our lives, about teachers ... " (quoted in Fernandes 2001: 113).

The process of questioning as a structural base for the pieces comes out of Bausch's growing confidence in her and her company's ability to enter in to material more indirectly. As Bausch explains, "[At first] I wanted everything prepared because I was scared. I was afraid somebody would ask me, 'What do I do?' and I would have to say 'I don't know'" (quoted in Manuel 1999: n.p.). But eventually, she is able to let go of those preparatory structures and open up new pathways to explore experience. "You have to just trust. We are there, the company and me, and life is there. And what do we do? We speak about life and love" (quoted in Manuel 1999: n.p.).

So now in rehearsal Bausch asks questions; questions of elemental purpose, allowing her performers time to answer with words, with movement, with a performed moment. "How do you cry?" A simple question, but built on different means than one expects in theatrical improvisation. Not "Why do you cry?" with all of its attendant psychological uncovering, but the more elusive "How?" She is looking for the way in which each individual contains his or her expression, how it lives in his or her body. Bausch uses tools of theatrical presentation to readdress the base assumptions from which interpretation arises, asking not only what moves us, but more specifically how we are

related to the question at hand both as performers and as people in the world. The means of presentation themselves are questioned, always reconsidering forms of presentation to reveal how we are involved in the process of performance.

In response to a question on how the work on her pieces begins, and whether the experiences she and her company collect find a home in the finished piece, Bausch answers:

> I can only make something very open. I'm not pointing out a view. There are conflicts between people, but they can be looked at from each side, from different angles. I don't know from where the piece comes. Even there, already something is there. It's not a picture, not a structure, but it has something to do with where you are in life at that period, the wishes, what you find scary.
>
> (quoted in Hoffman 1994: 12)

The early stages of shaping a piece, she says, "are very naked, very sensitive. The dancers have to be patient with me, to try to follow me" (quoted in Hoffman 1994: 12). The model of dance as people interpreting the unifying technique of a charismatic leader (modern dance), or a stable system of expression reinterpreted for each succeeding generation (ballet), is unsettled in favor of a highly collaborative effort, where all contribute their own experience toward the metaphoric construction of the whole.

The mode of questioning and exploration that the rehearsal process embodies draws on basic assumptions: a concentration on experience as the way we are connected to the world, and a prioritization of process over product and content over technique. The questions are posed to lead toward an uncovering of experience rather than the way that experience may be expressed, and that process is revealed in the performance. How do we exist on stage, and how do we use the stage to approach the way we are in the world?

Raimond Hoghe discussed with Bausch her role in rehearsal:

> During rehearsals Pina Bausch watches. She is very reticent with explanations to the performers. "I don't want to take your thoughts away from you," she says and encourages individuals to have their own imagination, to be more like themselves, to dare uncommon ways of thinking. "Just dare to think in all directions."
>
> (Hoghe 1980: 67)

The process is not nearly so efficient as crafting a preconceived pattern on a capable performer – it takes time. Bausch gives her dancers time to explore the (self-)questioning initiated by her, time to arrive at answers of their own.

> Very concentrated, very quietly she follows the quest of the group, the associations, proposals, histories of the various individuals. "What I do – watch," she says. "Perhaps that's it. The only thing I did all the time was watching people. I have only seen human relations, or have tried to see them and talk about them. That's what I'm interested in. I don't know anything more important."
>
> (Hoghe 1980: 68)

Bausch provides the stimulus for her dancers' explorations, and then stands back to watch and edit, push a little farther and look finally for a unifying thread on which the final performance might hang.

Bausch describes the beginning of rehearsals as follows:

> I find it incredibly difficult taking the first step because ... because I know they, the dancers, are then going to expect me to tell them what I want. And then I panic. I'm scared of having to tell them because what I have is often so vague. It's true, I know I can always say, "Here I am – there are one or two particular things in my head at the moment," and I might even find some kind of word to describe it and then I'll say, "Right. Well, here's where we start from. Lets see where it takes us."
>
> (quoted in Servos 2003, my translation: 309)

The initial idea comes out of the choreographer's and dancers' reaction to life, what's going on around them, and not just current events, but the very way in which they find themselves embedded in life and in their connection to others. The piece begins with a question. Schmidt asks Bausch: "Posing questions, has that become the point of departure for each work?" Bausch replies: "Yeah, that's what it always starts with. Everyone thinks it over and gives an answer. Sometimes it's got something to do with how its formulated, or with various things. Then we all take a look at them ... " Schmidt asks: " ... so the pieces do not begin, then, with a movement, but with a state of awareness, in the head rather than in the legs?" Bausch explains:

The steps have always come from somewhere else. They never came from the legs. And working on the movements – we always do that in between. And then we're always making little dance phrases which we keep in mind. In earlier days I may have started with a movement out of worry or panic, and dodged the questions. Nowadays I start with the questions.

(Bausch 1983b: 14)

Bausch watches and writes down everything. At first the performers had to rely on these scribbled notes to recall moments that Bausch wanted to bring back for further consideration, but more recently everything is videoed. Bausch then goes over the videos with the performers, making comments and asking them to repeat a moment, to join it with another from somewhere else in the process. The whole thing is incredibly laborious, with this first stage of exploration and collection of resources taking three months or more. During the process of gathering resources, Bausch also provides some movement patterns to be learned, or asks the performers to come up with specific movement-generated material. Movement days are interspersed with the catalogue of questions and responses until there is both a common base of physical language and an overwhelming array of individual responses to the questions of personal experience.

Describing the exploration that leads into rehearsals and the process for creating *Nur Du,* Bausch comments:

These weeks now, what we did, is just like finding material, just material. From this material, I'm using five percent maybe, and reworking it and doing it differently. And then we start to work on a piece. But I first create something which I can work with.

(quoted in Williams 1997: 76)

Long-standing company member Dominique Mercy continues:

She starts to ask questions. For instance, in one piece she says: "Tell me what you ate last night," or something to do with Christmas, or six different ways to be sad or angry, and of course with time, because this lasts quite a while, the questions become more complicated. Each time it's always your own experience. Even if you take things from the outside, it's the way you see them. It's yourself which is on stage.

(quoted in Williams 1997: 76)

When asked how answers to all of the questions fit together into a piece, Bausch responds:

> At first nothing fits together at all, and so you have this constant seeking further and collecting of material. During this time, of course, I work on other things as well. I take notes on everything; the dancers have to note down everything they do as well so that I can come back to them again later, and then I start sorting it all out ... That's where you have to keep totally alert, sensitive, receptive; there's no system.
>
> (Bausch 1995: 36)

So how does all that become a dance? How does the overwhelming volume of material get trimmed down and placed into a coherent structure? And why should that collaged structure be called dance? Bausch adds:

> That's ultimately the composition. What you do with the things. After all, at first it isn't anything. It's just answers – sentences, little scenes – which someone performs. Everything separate to start with. At some point or other, I combine something I thought right with something else. This with that, that with something else. One thing with various others. Then, when I've again found something that works, I've already got a slightly bigger little something. Then I go off somewhere completely else. It starts really small and gradually gets bigger.
>
> (Bausch 1982a: 235)

This becomes Bausch's version of choreography, taking these elements that have been derived in rehearsal from responses to questions that all push toward some underlying theme or central idea, and arranging them into evocative sequences and finally a crafted whole that works to uncover the core of the piece. The way the piece unfolds reflects the conditions of its creation, and just as the dancers are shifted from objectified movers, choreography is reoriented beyond the sequencing of steps to become the overall condition of the piece and the dancers' implicit bodily engagement in the event. The structuring element becomes that central focus, though it may no longer be the initial impression that began the process. Bausch explains:

> I have a lot of things, I don't know what they will become yet. Then, gradually, I begin to see where a work should start. What we have been working on is

usually a big mess of things – a big chaos of things, materials, in relation to the finished piece. For a while, I'm completely helpless. And I do more and more and more. Then suddenly, I have something that works, and I can start building the piece. I ask myself: How should it develop from that point? I start organizing the material. I work out from the middle. I cut those things – even when I like them – which don't fit, since the piece is moving in a different direction. Or because I saw the dancers do something new, interesting, I move the pieces in that direction. Sometimes it takes off in a different direction entirely, and then I have to find new materials. In rehearsals, suddenly some-body is so beautiful, so right, I have to take a chance on the idea and use that.

(Bausch 1985: 18)

The structural integrity comes out of dance principles and the individual moments come out of theater. It is an inversion of the traditional structure of story ballets, for instance, that use a movement-centered language to tell a theatrical story. In this case, we take moments of theatrical presence, and put them together through dance construction principles.

Our work is a mixture of elements. I don't know what it is. They dance; people talk; others sing. We use actors, too. And we use musicians in the works. It's theatre, really. For us, the stage – the settings – are important, too. We aren't just dancing in a room, in a space. Where it is, the location, the atmosphere where the movement happens, that matters in my works.

(Bausch 1985: 19)

Instead of being built on the dancer's body as empty vessel to execute the movement, the structure is built on the personal investment of the dancers. In working through this level of questioning and development from the performers, the final piece is bound to show not only Bausch's life, but the personal perspectives of the performers from whom she draws. The structure of the work is built upon the process of inquiry into our lives and our connection to the world, upon the private investigations of the choreographer and the dancers, made public. But getting at that individual investment is not always easy, as Bausch explains:

The dancers always want to answer the questions slightly differently than I ask. They are avoiding the question. So, I don't ask straight to the point because they are shy. It's a very delicate process.

(Bausch, 2004b, my translation: 11)

The process is able to move past self-indulgent centering on specific performers by concentrating on the more universal motivating impulse that stands as the base of the work. Asked if she is trying to uncover something within the dancers or herself, Bausch replies:

> Neither one. I want to find out something about us. Sometimes it's funny when you have to explain certain words. When someone asks what it means in Spanish. By trying to explain it you sometimes find out what you really want to know.
>
> (Bausch, 2004b, my translation: 11)

Christopher Bowen asked her if this might be a movement in late twentieth-century performance, people talking about their problems directly to the audience, but Bausch takes issue with the nature of that supposition.

> What we are doing is still abstraction. It is not a private thing; there are certain feelings that belong to all of us. If you are honest, it's not private, because we all know these feelings. We all have the same desires; we all are scared. There are differences – the taste, the flavor is different. But we are all together and it is the richness – all our possibilities – that I celebrate in my pieces.
>
> (Bausch 1999: 11A)

Each of Bausch's initial queries at the beginning of a rehearsal process goes through natural selection, with only those ideas that generated the most vital connection to the performers' concerns and struggles surviving. If most of Bausch's pieces end up concerning mainly human relationships, it is because that is what most concerns her dancers and herself. Her popularity and longevity would indicate that it most concerns her audience as well. Each performed moment relates back not to a formulated technique, or way of moving, but to our connection to others and to life. The content of the piece is the base from which all is generated.

PRESENCE – THE CENTER

Though the questions Bausch raises in rehearsal move toward universal experience, they all center on individual experience. Bausch asks her dancers, "What is your experience of – ?" with the blank standing for whatever the particular theme of the work in process might be.

Because the question of experience is posed with specific people in mind and with those same specific people answering, there is never any question of a performer's aptness to fit the part. This, in part, is what gives Bausch's performers such conviction: they are not performing a part, though they may address the idea of performing, they play themselves. Being themselves is called attention to on stage. Real names are used whenever the dancers address each other in performance. Which is not to say that we really see the people up there on stage; they are performing, and as such enter the roles they have created of themselves, and in so doing call into question and explore the very idea of role-playing.

This level of role-playing is made especially clear and further complicated as the company has transformed and new performers take on roles created by others as the older pieces are kept in repertory. As Ruth Amarante explains, the process of taking on someone else's role begins as a formal exercise, but because of the highly charged experiential work out of which the piece is generated, formal bounds soon collapse and the individual is once again asserted as the new performer claims the experience in performance. In describing her work on *1980*, she says:

> I joined this piece long after it was completed. I mean, I'm doing someone else's role. So, in the beginning it is quite formal. You have to be in the right tempo, you have to take care not to get into people's way, you have to get the chair in the right time, you have to do the movements – you have to do a bunch of things at the same time … After some time, you start relaxing and then getting the feeling; the thing starts to have a life of it's own.

> (quoted in Fernandes 2001: 114)

This is different than more traditional taking over of roles in long-running shows. Rather than projecting into a role as other and making it your own, the original history out of which the moment was derived begins to transform to contain the new performer. In explaining taking over a moment where the original performer describes a scene from childhood with her father, Amarante says:

> It is her history, but I take it for myself. So, it is as if it were mine. My father died a long time ago, too, so it is very related with the loss of a

close, dear person. It is not very far away. I incorporate the role of another
person like this.

(quoted in Fernandes 2001: 115)

The underlying feeling structure of the moment is made relevant to
the current performer and expressed as it is contained within her
body. It is made corporeal, incorporated into the present moment.

In rehearsals, the dancers try to mold their experiences into performed moments that Bausch will later recontextualize and rearrange
until something coalesces into what will be the final piece. "She wants
us," says Dominique Mercy, one of the longest standing company
members, "to be as sincere and simple as possible" (quoted in Daly
1996: 10). In response to a question on how all of the events the
dancers participate in and watch will translate into a piece about
America in *Nur Du*, Mercy continues:

the American commission should not be taken as literal or descriptive. The
point is much larger than the occasional flash of American imagery. There is
also something behind those specific experiences that speaks to larger issues
of human relations.

(quoted in Daly 1996: 20)

The pieces begin from and return to the central motivating impulse,
and that is always a feeling, an impression as it is experienced in
individual terms. Early pieces drew on outside sources as a base for
the underlying feeling that the work tries to contain, while those of
the fervent period of Bausch's reinvention of form were more open
explorations of feeling states. The pieces attend to a rhythm of
experience, a way of being in the world, and address more fundamental aspects of emotional experience. "There is something in here,"
she says, cradling her stomach. "But it has no words or pictures. I have
to find a way to discover the things I'm feeling. I don't make plans; it's
always open. Something suddenly happens. It's scary" (quoted in
Mackrell 1999: C1).

The pieces together can be seen as a whole, a continual process of
trying to uncover how we are placed in the world. As Bausch says:

I'm fighting for love, I'm fighting once again for love. I know what I want to say,
deep down inside I know that, in my mind. But I have the feeling I haven't

Figure 2.2 *Arien* (1979). Photo by Bettina Stöß

found it all yet. Sometimes there are moments when I feel something, when I know, "that's it, that's what I really mean." But it's still very small.

(quoted in Schmidt 1990: 43)

Each moment needs to be pushed toward its metaphoric connection to the underlying feeling. We are given access to our own feeling structures, as they are contained in our own base of being, but the door to this ground of feeling comes from the open metaphors derived from the company's own individual experience. Bausch explains:

I think it can only work if we avoid anything explicit – anything where we see something and we all know what it means. We think oh, this is a sign for that: you know it in your head. But if we avoid this and if the audience are open to experience or feel things, I think there is the possibility of another kind of language. It's not only choreography, but for me the stage is important, the space, the time, the music, the personalities; everything has to be brought together. It is not only a question of "Why do you not dance? Why do you do this?" Actually the reason is, I am interested in a certain feeling that I want to express, something there is no word for.

(Bausch 1992: 15)

The search for expression results in individual moments developed in rehearsal and all built on variations of the central thrust of the piece. When asked if all of those moments then add up to the feeling she wants, Bausch responds:

Yes, but it should not add up to "What did she think when she did this?" It is going to a different level than an intellectual level, it is a feeling – but a feeling which is very precise; it is not just some vague feeling, it is something absolutely precise. If you do it like this instead of like that, everything changes.

(Bausch 1992: 15)

The way in which the moments found in rehearsal come together in performance creates the underlying feeling structure for the piece, and that is interpreted from the base in the audience's own experience, now given concrete form. It is particular for each audience member, though there is a considerable area of overlap at the base structure of

what the performed moments contain. It is that area of overlap that Bausch's initial questions are seeking to expose.

IMPACT

The works are open metaphoric structures that tie us to the ground of our own being in the world. Through her questioning methodology and concentration on individual experience, Bausch creates open points of connection to more universal structures of feeling. It amounts to a new way of seeing, of opening up pathways of connection with the world. As Bausch explains:

> I think it is important to be confronted with reality, because we so often forget to look. When I go to our rehearsal studio between the peep show and the McDonald's, there is a bus station and all these sad people standing there. This is our entrance – One has to practice magic with one's work.
>
> (Bausch, 2004a, my translation: 10)

That process of uncovering has been in place from the beginning, and is in part what prompts the transition from more dance-centered works into tanztheater. Bausch doesn't set out to stake a claim in formal revolution against existing forms of dance, she simply concentrates on how we are connected to the world and how we feel what we feel. Her interest in what moves people rather than how they move is built on this fundamental base, and turns her away from the transporting illusion contained in previous forms.

> Very few people know what happens within themselves, why they have certain feelings, why they suddenly feel unhappy or content with themselves, why they go through periods of depression, etc. Can we afford to waste our time with "melodramatic diversions," as if we already cleared all our problems?
>
> (Bausch 1975, my translation: n.p.)

Any attempt at description of the work provides a surface level of what happened, but what really took place, took place inside me. The piece is felt more than perceived. My particular reaction, based in my own experience, is called up by the way the images tap into more elemental states. When I saw *Bandoneon* (1984), I saw the aura of dislocation the piece elicits from my own perspective. Having just

moved and being in a transitional time in my life, I felt the piece as a desire for connection and feeling outside of the physical tie to those I care about. While milling about at intermission, I overheard a woman remark to her friend, "I just started chemotherapy last week; *that's* how it feels." The woman spoke with a great deal of admiration for the performance and its ability to capture her experience. From outside the event, the piece is a series of rather brutal and disconnected images, but as this spectator entered the world of the piece, she was able to see the images from within her own experience.

The woman was open to the possibility of involvement necessary to complete the event. We both felt the sense of physical disassociation and desire for a more holistic entrance into life that the piece engendered. I understood those feelings from my own frame of reference, while this woman apparently was able to find those same feelings in her more physically immediate experience. The piece provided the ground and the resources and freedom for both interpretations.

Bausch draws on her own experience as well, as the responsive base from which the pieces spring forth.

> I look at myself as a normal person who reacts to everyday life just as everyone else does. I have to start from myself first, because I am the closest to myself, in my body and my heart. I am scared, content, I hope, just like everyone. Maybe this is why people react very strongly to my pieces, because they feel directly spoken to.
>
> (Bausch 1998, my translation: 19)

In a press conference Bausch gave in 1984 before the performance of some of her pieces at BAM, she said that the work starts small, with little moments of life, but the pieces are all finally "about the relationships between man and woman. The pieces are about how much we want to be loved. We are all afraid of death" (quoted in Smith 1984: 36).

The moments Bausch creates out of these personal experiences all reveal the underlying current that connects our experience. The images are not didactic, they don't tell us how to feel, but open up an experience into which we need to project our own meaning in order to complete, if meaning is what we are after. In *Gebirge* (1984), after a bout of frantic activity the performers all run off, leaving Jan Minarik silently standing over Beatrice Libonati, who kneels with her back to

the audience, making herself vulnerable. She pulls her dress up to her head, revealing her bare back. Minarik whips her with what we realize is lipstick in his hand, leaving a red streak down her back. After each lash with the lipstick, Minarik looks out to the audience for approval, waiting for someone to contradict, implying a kind of who's next? The woman does a slow ritualistic movement, head down, dress pulled out. She has big red marks on her back, they look horribly painful. Minarik walks away in silence, and the woman continues her ritual. We are left to decipher the image on our own, with only the other images of sexual oppression that surround it and our sense of and outrage at sexual violence to use as guideposts for interpretation.

Bausch is not trying to convince us of anything, so there is no felt morality. Because none is imposed on you, you have to find it within yourself. This, ultimately, is the goal of Bausch's approach to representation, to demand of the audience an inner search for a way to approach the images she unearths. Bausch is uncompromising in her display of the way we are connected to the world. She shows a harsh world in harsh terms. Your own response is either one of shock because you have isolated yourself from this reality or a feeling of connectedness in that you have struggled in this way too.

Rather than looking for a movement that might transport us, or a gesture that somehow captures authentic experience, tanztheater examines experience as it is lived in our daily connections to a larger culture and in our desperate search for connective meaning. It presents this experience as simultaneously real and metaphoric, for both the value of its real condition and for the larger truth to which it refers.

This means of representation exposes the theater as a place for the ongoing process of comprehending reality and creating self, rather than one where set meanings are given to an audience. Bausch forces us to question life and our placement in it, not by providing an alternative solution, but by providing a ground for exploration and a sense of the urgency of the problems she attacks.

In the preceding example of the woman whipped with lipstick, we must account both for the very real woman on stage going through what appears to be a horrid situation and for the larger idea of sexual oppression and violence to which her staged experience refers. The longed for resolving moments that might contain the stage image and keep it a part of the staged world are never provided. We must take

the unresolved tension with us to sort out each time we recollect the image, voluntarily or involuntarily. The contradictions of denying a resolving action that is acknowledged as desperately sought are fully recognized.

THE NEED TO ARTICULATE

Critic Anita Finkel claims that "Bausch will not allow us to deny nature, and we respond with anger. There are those who stay compulsively away from Bausch's theater because the spectacle of real flesh is too painful to bear, and they're right to absent themselves – once inside, Bausch's sense of the body as vulnerable is inescapable" (Finkel 1991: 4). Bausch also reawakens us to the reality of our bodies, and this is not always a disheartening experience, even for dancers who are most often reminded of the all too real nature of their bodies through injury or old age. Schmidt discusses *Waltzes*, perhaps the most optimistic of Bausch's early pieces, arriving after the birth of her son. She responds:

I don't want to sound banal, but really that [birth and motherhood] is a miracle. At the moment, I'm discovering things practically every day which seem almost inexplicable, quite incredible things. I suddenly see how things connect within my own body. You run around with a pair of breasts all your life and of course you know what they're for, but all of a sudden you feel their function. These are very simple things, I know. But it is a tremendous experience.

(Bausch 1982a: 235)

By reawakening us to our bodies and our bodily connection to the world and society, Bausch also reconnects us to our human relationships, doggedly so. Jochen Schmidt describes two facets of audience attraction and repulsion to Bausch; one being her insistent content:

Virtually all of the choreographer's pieces deal with those basic questions about human existence which anyone, unless he's merely vegetating, must ask from time to time. They deal with love and fear, longing and loneliness, frustration and terror, man's exploitation of man (and, in particular, man's exploitation of women in a world made to conform to the former's ideas), about remembering and forgetting. They are aware of the difficulties of human

co-existence and seek ways to reduce the distance between two (or more) individuals. They set out with a kind of brave desperation to develop a language with which to achieve the kind of communication that other languages and modes of speaking used up until now have failed to provide – and, if it's argued by some that all they've really produced so far have been piercing shrieks, that doesn't particularly disturb me; a work of art which shouts loud enough to shake people out of their lethargy is seldom enough.

(Schmidt 1984: 13)

The other facet of Bausch's art that Schmidt addresses

lies in the quality of mercilessness which everyone must feel in the way Bausch asks her existential, social, or aesthetic questions. The conflicts dealt with in the pieces are neither paraphrased nor harmonized, but fully acted out. Bausch makes no excuses nor does she allow the spectator to do so. To everyone, her critics included, she is a constant reminder of our own inadequacy, a constant annoyance, forever calling upon us to abandon routine and dullness, to throw off our coldness and to start trusting one another, respecting one another, showing consideration for one another as partners.

(Schmidt 1984: 13)

Our bodies, as defined by society and as our connection to society, provide the ground from which content naturally emanates. Bodily experience is the spring from which all else issues, showing tanztheater's growth from and connection to dance, but dance reconfigured. Dance becomes the aesthetic articulation of the means by which we define our selves through our own embodiment, and necessarily moves toward the theatrical. But theater is now re-enlivened with real presence made manifest through human bodies in time and space. Bausch is not the first to engage this type of presentation and expression, but she is the first to place that bodily presence at the center of her presentational praxis. Rather than for a constructed present, the performer is present, and that presence both creates and addresses our own sense of self intertwined with others. Our own connection to the world is shown as a bodily process, necessarily fractured, but what is important is not so much the gaps created between ourselves and others, but the persistence with which we try to bridge those gaps. We may be lonely in the world, but there is grace and hope in our attempts to achieve context.

A critic once remarked on one of Bausch's long-standing themes as "the impossibility of communication between the sexes" (*The Search for Dance* 1994: video transcription). I asked Bausch how she felt about that statement, and she responded, "Not impossibility. Difficulty. If it was impossible we would stop trying, but we don't. We keep trying, always, to find each other."

KONTAKTHOF IN CONTEXT

WHY *KONTAKTHOF*?

In the fall of 1985, I sat in the opera house at the Brooklyn Academy of Music in New York as the performers described at the beginning of the book made their way downstage in *Kontakthof*. They simply walked forward, with an odd hip thrust, confronting the audience in their march of presentation, looking straight at us, and I felt at me in particular, despite my seat halfway up the balcony. That direct gaze was exposing, and exposure always feels self-consciously personal. I had come to see this piece on the promise that it would be different. I was searching for a means to reconcile my theater education, my experience in dance choreography and theory, and what I dimly imagined possible on stage. The singularity of a reimagined presence I saw on Bausch's stage drew me in immediately, and I felt – though I still had no idea how to approach it – that here was an entrance into performance that opened up possibility. Since then, I have worked to try to uncover that presence; in my research, in my theater going, and in creating new works for the stage myself.

Kontakthof has been performed throughout the world over the past thirty years in the repertory of Tanztheater Wuppertal, with some of the original ensemble members who created the piece in 1978 and new performers taking over roles as the company shifts personnel. Bausch

also re-created the piece with a group of men and women over sixty-five in an amazing turn of the fragility and strength of performance presence. Each performer, whether the youngest new recruit to the company, or the older members of that intrepid group of senior citizens, stands before the audience and offers him or herself to the event. It is the sacrifice of self, the co-optation of strength through vulnerability, that we make whenever we step on stage, this time made palpable and used as a metaphor for our own lives. We look at these performers, and they dare to look back.

The look with which each performer confronts the audience recalls the glare of provocation, exposure, and visceral intensity of expressionist portraits. Austrian painter Egon Schiele (1890–1918), in particular, cleared a path into radical self-expression in his break from the more ornate surfaces of the style of portraiture that preceded him. He created perhaps the most jarring example in visual art of the expressionist attempt to uncover inner psychological truth. The connection between Schiele and Bausch is not so remote as one might think. Bausch's work continually picks up the threads of expressionist practice across the arts from the fervent period before the war. With this simple introduction to a piece about desire and connection (or the lack thereof), Bausch reclaims and extends earlier attempts at uncovering self-hood in performance.

As a representative example of Bausch's work, *Kontakthof* covers only a limited perspective, but it comes from a particularly important period in Bausch's development. Bausch's career has been varied and her scope large. Certainly, *Rite of Spring* (1975) stands as a testament to her dynamic choreographic style, and is the prime example of her early period with Tanztheater Wuppertal. Within the ballet world, it is regarded as a modern classic. But Bausch quickly shifted focus, and her reputation was built, primarily, from the creative period following the more dance-centered *Rite of Spring*, and in which *Kontakthof* is central. Her later periods all draw on that fundamental break in presentational practice. The pieces based on residencies that followed all take their basic constructive principles from methods established in the late 1970s. Even as the pieces shift focus again in more recent work from image-dominated collages to more movement-centered works, the basic approach to making a piece has not changed, and that approach was first systematically explored in the time around the creation of *Kontakthof*.

Re-setting *Kontakthof* on a cast of senior citizens gives us another perspective into the piece as well, and insight into the way in which Bausch's work in general operates on stage. Seeing the same desperate attempts at connection on older performers both implicates and alienates the audience from the events on stage. While you can never completely divorce the action from the context of its performance with either the original cast or this group of senior citizens, being able to place your response next to its counterpart on the other side of the performance equation offers a means of understanding how the images themselves work.

Because of its presence in the repertory, its re-creation with a still-touring ensemble of senior citizens, and its prominence in documentary coverage of Bausch's work, *Kontakthof* has become a central piece in defining Bausch's aesthetic. Or it could be central in my own understanding because it was the first piece of Bausch's I saw, eight years after its premiere. Whenever I ask people about their favorite Bausch piece, the answer that invariably comes up is the first piece of hers any given person has seen. The shock of first encounter with something that has the potential to refocus your own ideas often has lasting power.

But beyond my own response, *Kontakthof* stands as a central piece within the Bausch oeuvre. It takes the dramatic break in form enacted through work on *Bluebeard* and the *Macbeth* project and extends it into a full piece derived entirely from an open idea (in this case the limits and ramifications of tenderness), rather than a response to an outside source. *Walzer* (1982), created in this same period, does much the same thing, but has not lived on in repertory to the same degree, and while *1980 – A Piece by Pina Bausch* (1980) and *Bandoneon* (1980) were also created during this period and have toured a bit more, they don't have the same reimagined impact through performance by a different ensemble. Through its continual performance in its various presentations, *Kontakthof* has become an emissary for a new style of work. It gives us more variety of performance experience, more centrally located in the Bausch canon, than any other piece from Tanztheater Wuppertal. And it's my favorite, because I saw it first and because it changed my perspective on what was possible in performance.

COMING INTO BEING

Kontakthof is one of many of Bausch's pieces that investigate human relationships, specifically male/female relationships, but there is no

narrative story being told and no direct source material to reference or interpret. In the first weeks of rehearsal, the company simply starts with a vague collection of ideas about desire and connection. Bausch pushes into the idea of how we connect with each other, or at least how we attempt to connect. It begins with the idea of tenderness. "What is it? How does one do it? Where does it go? And how far does tenderness go at all? When isn't it tenderness any more? Or is it still tenderness?" (Hoghe 1980: 66). The point of departure is this group of simple questions. But close examination of these questions quickly reveals a wealth of associations and attitudes drawn from the dancers' own experience of connection in their lives.

The long rehearsal period begins by creating and gathering material. "Let's do something with our complexes," Bausch says. "We all have complexes, so let's demonstrate them. Everyone show what they don't like about their bodies" (quoted in Klett 1984: 13). From here, the company develops a presentational parade. They march up to Bausch in rehearsal and ask to be considered. It's a form of audition, but also stands in for any moment of offering yourself up for judgment, on stage, and in life.

They try creating an image that is later dropped where each performer literally reveals a bit of him or herself; a shoulder, the small of the back, navel, or sole of the foot (see Klett 1984: 14). The questions about tenderness and the exploration of connection begin to center on these moments of presentation. In another section that they call "The Museum," "everyone stands around as if at a party, until someone falls down, throws up, smashes against the wall. The others watch, indifferent or interested, as if looking at a work of art instead of a person" (Klett 1984: 14). The moments created by the performers in rehearsal gradually coalesce around ideas of connection and what we do to get it. How we exhibit ourselves in the attempt to be noticed and what we do with and to each other once a point of connection has been reached.

The performers use the resources at hand to develop this growing catalog of images; their own lives, the developing context of the 1950s (primarily established through the music that underscores each action, a series of sentimental love songs from the era), and the idea of presentation in the theater itself.

As the amount of images created in rehearsal grows, Bausch begins the equally long process of selection and ordering. How one moment

leads into the next begins to create pathways that expose different aspects of the images and also leads to new material. It all must be sifted and sorted to create the overall impression of the piece. When Renate Klett, acting as a rehearsal assistant, suggests various threads to follow that fit more expected ideas of story and character development, Bausch finds it boring. It leads to a too simplistic version of the pieces and the audience cannot find their own entrance into the material. Klett explains Bausch's structural method:

> She doubles scenes, complicates their structure by intermixing them. Many scenes run parallel, commenting on and overlapping each other. Sometimes ten different actions occur at once; then again everything is concentrated on one single event.
>
> (Klett 1984: 16)

The effect Bausch is striving for is a web of impressions that an audience can enter into from their own perspective. The work comes from the individual responses of Bausch and her performers and should be open to the personal investment of the audience.

Once the final construction of the piece begins to fall into place, they look for a title that might be specific enough to elicit the underlying ethos of the piece, but open enough to allow for a variety of interpretations. After going through a long list of possibilities, they arrive back at *Kontakthof*, which Bausch had suggested early in the process. In German, "Kontakthof" literally means meeting place, and is usually used to refer to a courtyard or square, as in a prison or a school, but it can also refer to a place where prostitutes meet their clients, where the body is offered for sale. Theater as a kind of prostitution is explored throughout the piece; a place where contact is expected, where the performers offer themselves to "the mute expectancy of the audience waiting to be impressed" (Servos 1984: 117).

Bausch begins the rehearsal process by approaching content, by asking "What is connection? How do we go about it?" What makes it through the exhaustive developmental process are those images that reflect the base of her and her performers' experience. They may start with something specifically personal, but the transition into moments of performance entails moving past the surface detail and into the underlying energy from which the idea or feeling comes. The world of the theater is one of the metaphors she finds for the expression of this

basic human conundrum of desire for and difficulty in maintaining connection. Bausch simply took what was at hand – her dancers' experience in theatrical techniques – and made them work on a metaphoric rather than on a literal level.

PERFORMANCE

The setting for *Kontakthof* is a large room with walls on three sides, a few simple doors upstage right and left, and a large vertical window on the stage right wall. There is a stage in the back with a black curtain, an upright piano in the corner and simple black wooden chairs lining the walls. It resembles a meeting hall (or the "Lichtburg," a remodeled movie theater that the company uses as a rehearsal space). It is a particularly bland and open environment, meant to highlight the presentation of the performers to come. The setting is the stage itself and creates an arena for action rather than an illusion-istic world into which we might invest, though it does lend a sense of its worn placement in a vague post-war time period to the tenor of the piece. Bausch's settings – from her early collaborations with Rolf Borzik of which this is a part, to her work with Peter Pabst since Borzik's death in 1980 – are places where things happen, often with one dominant reverberant element that dramatically influences how the performers exist in that space, whether that is the dirt covering the floor in *Rite of Spring* or *Gebirge*, water in *Arien*, or flowers in *Nelken*, and so on. The goal is to let the stage be as open a structure as possible, but with a particular feeling that permeates the piece and helps color the action.

Music also plays an important structural as well as emotional role in most of the pieces. It is almost always a vast range and collection of material that underscores both movement and imagistic moments, and that subtly carries the weight of an imagined context with it. In this case, the music is mostly a mix of popular German songs from the 1930s through to the 1950s, with a few other pieces added in for particular moments. At least from an American perspective, I recog-nize the style of the music and easily place the tone within this time period, but I don't specifically recognize any of the songs. The music helps create the web of impressions that the piece becomes, but is never so specific as to limit meaning to one particular interpretation. I see the music as nostalgic and sentimental, a world before my time,

and at least in its original presentation with the main group of company members from Tanztheater Wuppertal, I imagine it has a similar connotation for most of the audience and the ensemble.

When presented with the cast of senior citizens, however, the music suddenly changes focus and becomes a more specific reference to the world of these performers. I imagine them listening to this very music at a meeting hall perhaps quite similar to the one depicted on stage, ever hopeful of a moment of connection amidst the quiet guilt and rebuilding of post-war Germany.

Because I know these are not professional performers in the senior citizens' performance of the piece, I am brought into a different relationship to their presentation of self. Even though their roles are constructed for this performance, there remains a strong influence of the actual person in the creation of character that the performers enact. That same presentation of self is in place with the regular ensemble as well, because I know that the images they present are derived from their own experience, but it is highlighted with the senior citizens.

The presentation of self we see in *Kontakthof* is an extension of the theatrical nature of display pulled out and used for dramatic and metaphoric purpose, and that becomes a leitmotif in many of Bausch's pieces. What does it mean for us to put ourselves up here to be looked at for the next few hours? In *Kontakthof*, that sense of offering yourself up for critique and the balance of power and vulnerability that is implied in that gesture is developed metaphorically as a link to our search for love and connection. In other cases the purpose changes with the context, but in all the ground remains the performers' own experience. We are not allowed to pretend that these people are anything but performers on a stage, and that role in itself is used for dramatic purpose.

The piece begins with the performers all seated in the chairs lined up at the back of the stage. The women wear an array of colorful cocktail dresses, while the men are in suits. They sit in their chairs and look at the audience impassively. One woman in a red dress walks downstage and stops before the audience. She turns around to show us her back, returns to face us and puts her hands behind her head. She opens her mouth to show us her teeth, then turns to the side. She drops her hands to show us her palms and then the backs of her hands, before turning around and walking back to rejoin the group seated upstage. Another woman comes forward and repeats this procedure, and then another. A man comes forward and also repeats this

Figure 3.1 *Kontakthof* (1978). Photo by Bettina Stöß

Figure 3.2 *Kontakthof with Ladies and Gentlemen over 65* (2000). Photo by Jean-Louis Fernandez

series of actions while the first song ends. The song speaks of longing: "Frühling und sonne schein, bist du allein" ("Springtime and the sun shines, but you are alone"). Another man comes forward while another song begins. All the men come forward and perform the ritual of presentation and, as the women come to join them, the men leave. The women are left alone and all go through the act of presentation.

The performers present themselves as property to be examined as if for sale, and we are the ones making the purchase. The performers cannot escape themselves in this transaction, they offer their bodies to us to be looked at, to be deemed worthy. But they are able to stand aside from the roles they create as well. The performed characters of the dancers both acquiesce and subtly stand in defiance to this commodification. They allow it to happen, but the confrontational and pained expression they project makes the audience aware and uncomfortable with their own implicit involvement in the objectifying practice.

Beyond the objective context that this moment makes real, this image shows the extent to which we are all involved in societal approval for who we are as bodies. The dancers ask for our approval before they continue on their mating ritual, and show the process by which we all constantly check our value within a society that highlights body image. The dancers call attention to the use of their bodies within dance or theater itself, but the process by which they are valued within the society of performance is also a comment on the more general body valuing that goes on in life, and particularly in the search for relationships. The context of the rest of the piece – where various performers offer themselves as wares within the context of male/female relationships – makes this point clear. Norbert Servos analyzes this opening moment as follows:

> The body is merchandise which must be appropriately displayed in order to fetch a decent price, whether in personal or professional life. The apparently private sphere of the individual body is shown to be subject to the same laws as the public person. In this respect, the reality of the dancer who must market his body and his technique is no different than that of the audience. Both must sell themselves and control their affects in line with prescribed codes.
>
> (Servos 1984: 118)

The dancers are placed in a given context and act within the societally prescribed norms of their situation. They uncover the posturing and

display inherent within our social system, and act in accordance with the paradigm in which they are enmeshed.

Kontakthof uses techniques of theatrical presentation as metaphors for the general idea of presentation and connection in our social relationships. Simply and dramatically the act of presentation in the theater is acknowledged and made meaningful. One woman speaks, "Good evening, I'm from Paris." And another, "I'm from Hamburg and I'm married." Each offers a short phrase of identification. They introduce themselves to us as one might at a party, but the presentation is always self-consciously theatrical, with the performers directly addressing the audience. After the women have all introduced themselves, they turn to join the line forming upstage, with the last woman slyly looking back over her shoulder at us again before she joins the group. Now they all come forward en masse, with a brush of the foot, thrust of the hip, and two steps in time with the music. The men join in and the whole group comes at us in waves, retreating downstage to repeat the traveling action every time they reach the end of the stage.

Finally, they stand in silence, looking out at the audience. One woman shakes her head, laughing hysterically, until she collapses on

Figure 3.3 *Kontakthof* (1978). Photo by Bettina Stöß

the floor. The others barely register her violent action. After a little more silence, a man begins singing slowly, and the group gradually disperses with the same brush-hip-step-step traveling action back to their seats upstage, leaving the collapsed woman on the floor alone. Someone screams and they all run off, except one woman who runs and screams as a man chases her, throwing a mouse at her feet at every turn, eliciting another scream. Another song begins and the women enter and walk awkwardly on their heels in a line that moves diagonally across the stage.

Throughout this opening section, every action is done for someone else, whether for each other on stage or for us in the audience, and there is a sense of expectancy with each action. It is as if the performers are continually asking, "Is this what you wanted to see?" or doing something, anything, to try to elicit a response. After a moment of silence, a woman slowly enters and plays one high note on the piano. She squeals. She plays another lone low note and moans, but before this image has a chance to develop, the music is back, along with the line of women moving in unison, this time awkwardly adjusting their bras, underwear, or pantyhose. They march across the stage in awkward regimented unison. A woman sits on a man's lap at the back and then does a little dance for him. As the procession of undergarment adjusters continues, the woman coos to the man, "Oh – you're so handsome. Ooo – you're so strong." She tries to get his attention with little coy movements, but the man simply turns around and exits. Another couple has entered and gently touches each other. Little timid, flirtatious touches that continue while a pair of women at the back whisper to each other, their caustic comments amplified by a microphone:

> "That dress is a bit tight around the waist."
> "She's gotten so fat."
> "She has. I mean she looks like the side of a house now."
> "Such flabby old skin."
> "Old skin, and it's real soft. It hangs on her."
> "Just hangs on her arms and chin."
> "It's like a mask."
> "And the make-up!"
> "Oh, the make-up, but if she didn't have that much on, I mean what would she look like?"

Meanwhile, a man has entered with a clipboard and takes notes. The actions are overlapped and it's easy to get lost amidst all of the activity. The specificity of each action is not what is important, but the way they all come together to create an overall feeling of relationships, thwarted desire, and calls for attention. The energy is carefully calibrated as well, with actions orchestrated to move between raucous group activity and smaller quiet moments between a few people. As open as the structure appears, we are carefully being led on a journey into the heart of this world.

The performers all have moments of emphatic self-presentation, always in desperate search for connection. One woman enters the empty stage and stands on a chair. She says, "I'm standing on the edge of the piano and I'm about to fall. But before I fall I scream, loud, so that nobody misses it." She screams and the rest of the performers run on and take their seats. The woman gently gets down from the chair and crawls under it. She says, "Then I crawl under the piano, look around, and act like I want to be alone. But I don't really want to be alone. Then I take my scarf and try to strangle myself, hoping someone will come before I die." As we watch the succession of images, they begin to reverberate off each other, coloring the way we see each succeeding moment. This woman uses her body as bait to receive the attention of others and the similarity between this type of gesture and the more common dressing up and display of the body in an attempt to lure someone into connection is demonstrated by their juxtaposition. Both approaches sacrifice the subject in an attempt to reach the other through objective manipulation.

After the woman's attempt to gain attention, the group runs on and begins a frantic push downstage, again coming at us in waves and retreating upstage to come again after each approach. Two people are screaming at each other across the stage and one man deliberately lies down and stays there as if he is dead. Some of the performers simply stand and stare out into the audience, and amidst this organized chaos, a woman enters with a microphone and performs little cries of ecstasy. The other performers stop and applaud and the woman looks to them for approval. She continues her performance while the others congregate in a semicircle. After another round of applause she rejoins the group to let someone else have a turn. Dancers move to the center in pairs and display little gestures of physical abuse. A man pokes a woman in the breast. The group applauds. The woman undoes

the man's pants and pulls them down. The group applauds again. Another couple moves to the center and the woman hugs the man while grinding her heel into his foot. The man caresses and then flicks the woman's nose. Several couples proudly perform their little tortures to the group's applause, until the music changes and the group disperses.

The men all run to one side of the stage and sit and the women run to the other. They frantically gesture to each other across the vast space. The men move their chairs forward in little runs, gradually getting closer to the women standing against the wall, all the while gesturing frantically. Eventually they are on top of each other in couples, still gesturing frantically beyond their partners so that their hand and arm motions become slaps and flailing attacks. As the music changes the couples begin a swinging dance, with the men carrying the women around the stage. Jan Minarik, the man with the clipboard at the beginning, walks around the stage with a tape measure and takes measurements from each couple – an inseam, the distance between one couple's faces – and duly writes his findings in his notes.

The connections that occur appear haphazard, with various people drawn together as dancing partners because that is what the dance requires rather than there being any coherent character or story-based reasoning for the partnering. The world that is developed is one of the need for connection in and of itself, without regard to the quality of connection that might be obtained. As the images continue, we do get a sense of individuals in the group based on their particular actions, but never is that a basis for an imagined connection. Jan Minarik, however, does create a particularly individualized character. He stands apart from the rest of the group, as he often does in Bausch's pieces from this time, as a kind of master of ceremonies. He always seems to be carrying around a microphone to bring out some particular couple's speaking, or a camera or tape measure to catalog the events as they take place, jotting down his findings on his clipboard. He is the ethnologist carefully transcribing the mating rituals of this particular group of human animals. But he enters into the action as well. He is the one who throws the mouse at the screaming woman, for instance, always hoping for a response and getting what he wants as she runs and giggles through the same pattern every time he returns to his mouse throwing.

A coin-operated children's horse is brought on stage while a woman works to teach a man a hip-swaying movement across the floor. She says, "Can you show me that step one more time? Wait a minute, hold your jacket up or I can't see anything." The man tries to rotate his hips in steps that travel downstage, but the woman interrupts him. "That's not right at all. Here." She demonstrates. "Circles, circles, circles. You're just doing this and this. That's not right at all." As the man tries to produce the action, the woman continues to berate him before finally leaving in disgust, saying, "Do it properly, I know you can do it. Keep working on it." The whole group enters and all move downstage with huge smiles and wide hip circles in time to the music, the original man desperately trying to keep up and watching others to see if he is doing it right.

This act of teaching movement, and the general objectifying tone that comes with it, makes regular appearances on Bausch's stage. She often uses images that refer more directly to the rigorous ballet training that most of her ensemble members have endured, and the feeling of inadequacy that often accompanies such trials in the rehearsal studio where you feel that your body betrays you and will not do what your mind knows it should. The act of physical training that some dance employs literally separates our sense of self from our bodies, particularly in ballet where any sense of self is obliterated in the need to make movement present. Here, that feeling is added to the body presentation and attempts at connection that make up the rest of the piece.

When the regular ensemble performs this image, we see it in the context of their extensive dance training, but when the senior citizens perform, this kind of image appears particularly brutal and dehumanizing, before ultimately becoming triumphant. We know that these untrained performers have worked hard to be able to accomplish this piece, and to see that work placed under this scrutiny feels especially harsh. But I do judge the older dancers on their ability to do the movement, despite my not wanting to evaluate them on that level. The conditions of performance dictate my response, just as social structures dictate my response to bodies in life. But in this context, I am often amazed at the older performers' ability to match the conditions of movement imposed on them by the piece. The simple act of triumph over the material becomes an exultation.

As the group disperses, a woman comes down to the audience to ask for change. After receiving a quarter she goes to the coin-operated

horse, puts her money in, and climbs into the saddle. The woman sits expectantly, but the horse doesn't move. She gets off the horse and goes back to the audience for more change. When she gets another quarter, she goes to the horse and tries again. She still has hope that maybe this time the horse will respond, but still nothing. She gets off the horse with an air of resignation and dejectedly returns to the group. After the whole group goes through a series of sensual gestures, a man takes the woman back to the horse and shows her that it was not plugged in. Some crew members come out with an extension cord and once the horse is plugged in, the woman gleefully goes back to the audience looking for more change. After getting another quarter, she scurries back to the horse, deposits her coin, and jumps on for the horse's lurching, hesitant ride. Another woman leaves the group and stands waiting for her turn on the horse, and then another until there is a line of women waiting for the horse, while the rest of the group continues with their gestures which have now turned to more violent pokes and tweaks, lifts, and carries.

This ballet of body posturing and attempted connections continues in a succession of overlapping images. Bausch is relentless in her exploration of the degree to which we objectify ourselves in our search for connection, and the ultimate futility of this objectification leading to anything more substantial than momentary attention. In the end, the women get more satisfaction from the horse than they ever do from any of the men in the piece. Beyond the direct reference of the mechanical horse as a metaphor for satisfaction (in both a sexual and an emotional capacity), we are also treated to the sheer joy of the image itself. To see these women ride this sadly rocking horse is both poignant and funny. You can look for what it "means," or you can just enjoy the image in its absurd aptness to the situation and context that exists on stage at that moment.

A bit later, a man and a woman sit facing each other at either side of the stage. They begin shyly and meekly gesturing to each other across the huge expanse. Slowly, they begin removing their clothing; first their shoes, then their socks, shirts, and so on, until finally they sit naked, still gesturing across the space. The other dancers have meanwhile formed a rigid line that circles about the stage in a unison march. Once the man and the woman are fully undressed, the line of marchers, who had been ignoring them up to that point, stop and glare at the couple and then act embarrassed. The couple, like Adam

and Eve suddenly aware of their nakedness, cover themselves, run out, put on their clothes hurriedly, and join the group. The actions are precisely visceral, with the delicacy of the couple's gestures and the vulnerability of their undressing in opposition to the formality of the group's march, and we see this couple's attempt at connection brought under the control and dominance of the group.

The image is further heightened and made more complex in the version performed by people over 65 years old. The same sense of shame and awareness in the attempt at connection through a moment of shared intimacy is there, but added to this is the uncomfortable sense of just how vulnerable these performers become. In the original version the performers maintain a strength of presence in revealing their well-toned bodies, but in the latter version, we are made aware of how we are supposed to view our bodies as betraying us at certain points in our life. The performers are beautiful in a simple and exposed way, but I couldn't escape feeling complete sympathy for these people going through an event that must have made them very uncomfortable. That feeling itself showed me how much we incorporate an antagonistic relationship to our own bodies throughout our lives, and especially as we age and are supposed to keep such things hidden.

The orchestration of these various images all lead us to the couple quietly undressing across the space, and that provides a kind of an ending as we go to the first of two intermissions. Even as intermission is announced, the action on stage continues in small ways, and I can never completely escape the world I have entered when I came into the theater. It was never a world I could simply watch from the outside to begin with, but an environment in which I am complicit, and I am made aware of my own engagement in the piece. I take it with me as I go out to the lobby and feel a bit self-conscious as I watch those around me, imagining that they see through me in the same way that I think I can see through them. We are all sad and hopeful, calling for attention and trying not to be noticed. I see it in the clothes I wear, the way I cut my hair, and the book in my pack that I will read on the subway on the way home.

Coming back from the intermission, the performers are all dressed in black and moving in a circle, all performing a series of small gestures in time with the music. The women peel off, leaving the men to saunter around the space with their gestures, and as the women return back in their colorful dresses, the groups confront each other.

A man calls out "Back! Stomach! Knee!" and the women retreat starting from a sharp action from the body part that has been called out, as if they have been shot in that particular place. A woman responds with commands of her own, "Hand! Cheek! Back!" and the men take their turn in injured retreat in this battle of the sexes. The traded assaults come faster and become more insistent until the two groups stop in frozen opposition. The men take off their coats and the women their shoes. The men all muss their hair and the women drop their hands on their heads. As the group moves toward each other and the couples separate into antagonistic pairs again, poking and tweaking at each other, Jan brings out a chair and sits to watch.

The images continue, some repeated from before, some new. The ensemble lines up their chairs facing the audience and all talk at once. Jan makes his way down the line with a microphone and we hear snippets of conversations about relationships in English, French, German, Spanish. All the conversations I understand (the ones in English and those in German when they speak slowly enough for me to keep up, which isn't often) are pointless moments between men and women as if in an endless phone conversation. The images build and I am able to move more freely amongst them now, seeing details I may have missed the first time, remarking on how different people enter in to the different scenarios. I move in the midst of the work as if it were a dream that keeps showing me how it feels to want, and I carry that dream with me from sitting here in the house to the lobby at intermission, to recalling the images years later.

Another chaos of action, people running, dancing, little screams of ecstasy, a man plays the piano, couples waltz, some sing along with the music, until finally someone sings "My Bonny Lies Over the Ocean" and gradually everyone joins in. It becomes a nice chorus before everyone gets quiet and we hear one woman at the back quietly weeping through the song: "Oh bring back my bonny to me." The rest of the ensemble quietly exit, leaving the crying woman at the back. A woman comes and joins the crying woman (to offer some support?) and then everyone comes downstage and sits with their backs to the audience. The curtain across the back is pulled open revealing a screen and someone brings on a movie projector. The lights dim and we all watch a short film about ducks and their mating habits ("a small happy brood of mallards"). It has the tone of a school informational film. When it finishes, there is a small groan of disappointment from

the entire group before people disperse and a woman comes to ask for more change for the mechanical horse.

The images all begin to blur together and there is an overall feeling of fatigue, whether mine or the performers' or some combination of the two, it's impossible to say. The performers, all dressed in black now, stand at various positions around the stage. Couples slowly come together, and Jan takes their pictures. As the woman who was chased by the mouse at the beginning comes back, Jan chases after her again and once again throws his mouse. The woman does not react. She follows the same pathway she did before, up on chairs, across the stage at the back, but does it all in deadpan slowness, unfazed by the mouse, until Jan, disappointed, walks off. The woman stops and stands facing front.

After two hours and forty-five minutes of alternatively harrowing and touching moments, we are left with this woman standing and looking at us. She wears a white dress and black shoes and simply stands downstage center. She addresses the audience with her blank gaze and invites consideration. She provides no outward expression for us to receive. Gradually one man and another and another approach her and begin to caress her; rubbing her shoulder, stroking her cheek. I supply the meaning for these gestures and receive the warmth of the touch, wanting the woman to mirror my expected response of opening up to the attempted connections. But the woman remains passive. By subverting my expectation of tender response, the piece strips me of my interpretive clothing and I am left to be re-clothed in the image.

Gradually the men's gestures become more mechanical, moving from the warmth of a caress to the gentle prod of awakening to the investigative delving into a foreign object. At what point does tenderness turn into cruelty? The limp woman is now surrounded by men, held up and shaken, her hair is smoothed, her face pinched, hand held up, all in a flurry of randomly repetitive motions. The woman's body has become object, and I must continually remind myself of the person in there somewhere going through what has now become a torture.

This "manhandling" continues long after I have grown uncomfortable with it. I soon, however, find my discomfort move into acclimation. I get used to the activity and ignore the objectifying and rather brutal implications. But the image continues, and soon I find myself uncomfortable with myself for my own placidity. I have been

implicated because I allow this to continue. Of course I am contained by my passive presence in the audience, this is no call to audience participation, but I am made to realize how I take on the role of passive enabler in life.

It is this implicit involvement that suddenly brings the image to light, for me. To say that men objectify and abuse women even through the subtlety of their actions is a nice point. But to say that this process continues and we get used to it, that we remind ourselves and then forget again, that the process is so continual that we must constantly awaken ourselves to the screaming of the silent, unmoved woman, is a provocative and disturbing indictment of contemporary culture.

The men continue their prodding for what seems like an eternity (actually six minutes), until another woman enters and the men all move to follow her as she seductively leads them into a circle, leaving the tortured woman alone. The other women come out to join the circle and the full group walks in unison, all performing the same simple gestures, with their audible footsteps continuing after the music has ended. The lights go out, leaving only the sad thump, thump, thump of the dancers' footsteps as they continue their circle dance. The heartbeat of the group continues after everything; a sad commentary on our ability to ignore even the most brutally objectifying images in our desire to belong, and our necessary connection to and definition through the group.

But that is an intellectual response I derive after the performance. For the moment sitting there in the dark I am stunned, oddly uncovered, and exhausted. Bausch has made us all work hard, and the penultimate image of that woman lingers. I see her in my mind and carry the image with me as I head back out into the lobby. Despite the artifice of the situation, the woman goes through a very real event, and her presence on stage is a product of both her actual existence in this moment, and the long and dense collage of images that lead up to it. The moment has power, in part, to the degree that we are able to see the woman as a real person enduring a real as well as a metaphoric trial, and Bausch has supplied a context that demands our attention to her subjectivity as expressed in bodily terms. She incorporates, or makes body, the underlying feeling structure of the image because it is enacted on her and expressed with the real presence of her body in the moment.

Beyond this particular moment, the way in which this process of incorporation works throughout the piece was never so clear as in the remounting of *Kontakthof* by the group of senior citizens. What before was the rather desperate longing and lack of connection as performed by the original company is not altered in its surface details (in fact the specificity with which this new ensemble is able to re-create the details of the original production is astounding), but the way the piece reads changes drastically. We see a hard-won resolve and acceptance in the older performers that realigns our own conception of desire away from the active push contained in the original performance. The older performers still push in their seemingly fruitless search for meaningful connection, but that push takes on a pathos previously absent and made all the more palpable when placed in bodies that belie the youthful intent inherent in the piece.

I felt as if I could suddenly see the attempt to reclaim the youthful presence contained within each person on stage, and I was forced to move them out of the bounds under which I might normally contain them. It was like seeing my mother at her fiftieth high-school reunion, playing through the dynamics of youthful romance from a remove and

Figure 3.4 *Kontakthof with Ladies and Gentlemen over 65* (2000). Photo by Jean-Louis Fernandez

reinventing that part of herself long hidden in her many years as wife and mother, the only means of definition I had previously had to understand her. I am forced to see these people under new conditions. It is a moment of Brechtian alienation taken to the extreme and shot through the piece as an overriding metaphor for our own distance from life. The performers create the world on stage through a combination of actual presence and metaphor rather than telling us something, or giving us a story with characters that we can understand and leave when we exit the theater.

Many ask why the woman in this final moment doesn't speak out, doesn't take action to stop the tweaks and pokes of the men. But if she were to use her free will to act against the objectifying gestures of the men, the situation would change and her being would change with it. She would reclaim her being and force us to consider her under new guidelines, and those new guidelines let me off the hook. If the woman acts, then I can see her as a dynamic feminine presence, in charge of her world and able to stand against the objectifying male behavior that surrounds her. I can cheer for her as she responds to the men who are not me, because I don't do those things. But her stillness and tolerance signify something else. Her body, in this case, both situates her in a very real moment and serves as the ground for a metaphor, pushing past this particular situation to comment on a larger reality. Again, we have an image of the plight of women in contemporary culture, where women fight to move beyond the cultural projections in which they find themselves entrapped. Her resistance is implied, but she is helpless to act, and I cannot escape my own complicity in the moment and the need to reawaken myself to the way I may unthinkingly contribute to an objectifying culture.

Bausch makes explicit the abuse and repression that each woman carries implicitly within her body. A woman need not go through specific abuse to incorporate this process of objectification, it is enough that the culture in which she is situated and out of which she constructs her being contains the process of abuse and repression as a dominant influence. A woman walking alone on a dark street, or entering a male-dominated workplace, need not ever have been specifically assaulted to have the potential for assault invade her being within that context, thereby changing her bodily presence. And I certainly don't have to act abusively in order to be perceived as a threat walking down that same dark street. Responses to abuse and

repression have been learned and express themselves through each individual woman's bodily presence in context. Bausch points to that process of incorporation and reawakens the actual abuse latent within the woman's bodily being. And, as stated, the process continues and we forget, only to be awakened again. I want to forget this process of abuse and objectification and my own implication in the event, but Bausch won't let me forget.

The woman expresses what Ann Daly calls "the unheard rage of a woman" (Daly 1986: 54), as well as the desire to move out of the projections of others. If she were to act against the process of objectification she would provide the audience with a desired sense of resolution, carrying away our own feelings of involvement and implication in our identification with her. Many people find Bausch disturbing precisely because she does not give the audience that easy release, but forces us to confront our own projections by leaving the situation unresolved. We are left to consider our own involvement in the process of objectification we see before us and, by implication, larger processes of objectification that surround us in our lives. Bausch points out the implicit abuse that continually haunts women, and the desire to escape it.

I left the theater unsure how to approach other people, but feeling the need to find a sympathetic hand and hold it. The piece, finally, is the collection of images as a whole, and Bausch's choreography is the subtle interlacing and orchestration of those images that lead me from one moment to the next. Something happens in Bausch's theater, and I feel I am a part of it. Others may not feel the same connection, or may willfully avoid it, but for me, and a growing audience world wide, Bausch creates an environment of interaction. My idea of performance has shifted and my connection to the world deepened.

COMING TOGETHER

Looking back on the piece, *Kontakthof* combines two elements that become central to Bausch's work: the redefinition of bodily presence on stage and a dream structure that carries us through the piece. Both are vital to the reimagination of performance practice that Bausch's pieces show us. We see the performer as more than either a created character or a moving body. People on Bausch's stage are expressive in and of themselves, and as they exist physically within the performance

arena, and that arena is constructed through overlapping metaphoric images that unearth deeper structures of feeling, much like dreams.

The dancer's body in Bausch's work always exceeds the bounds of movement any performer enacts, and the presence that is developed enforces our seeing past the movement to the person underneath and cultural codes as they are incorporated. The reality of the dancer's body on stage is given increasing importance, rather than some abstract ideal of movement the dancer tries to emulate. Even more, the bodily attitudes the dancers enact are drawn from the social fabric in which our image, and indeed our sense of self, is enmeshed. Our bodily relation to society is explored, in terms of both our placement within the structure of society and the longing to find some sense of true definition beyond that realm.

In *Kontakthof*, the dancers' bodies are displayed objectively as empty postures used either to lure a partner, or as the material presented to the audience. Even as we see past this objective structure, we are made aware of its dominant influence in performance practice. I left the theater with an uneasy feeling of participation in a ritual sacrifice, where, perhaps for the first time, I was made aware of the negation of self expected within the theatrical process where performers either ask me to invest in their portrayal of character (as separate from themselves) or erase themselves in the attempt to make movement the central mode of expression. Bausch counts on the audience needing to look past the dehumanizing aspects of self-presentation she displays to find the human element behind the theatricalized experience. She does not allow the audience to lose sight of reality through either technical virtuosity (though the dancers are all technically proficient, the scenarios they create on stage don't call attention to that fact) or the alluring completeness of a created world on stage (though the world that is created is precisely crafted).

The images we are shown are deliberately open-ended and demand that we turn to our own experience and a consideration of the dancers' experience beyond the created environment in order to give the performed metaphors meaning. The performances' strengths lie in this constantly shifting awareness within each individual audience member between what they are presented, how they relate to it personally, and how they can then reinvest that awareness back into the theatrical experience. The dancers do not re-present experience bodily, but begin the process whereby bodily experience is made present. That

realigned attitude toward the performer's body on stage provides a base for a new approach to performance and creates an alternative to either illusionistic practice in theater or abstract movement for movement's sake in dance.

The other aspect of performance practice Bausch explores is dream construction. In our dreaming world, we reorder our experiences along metaphoric structures. Dreams bring us to a particular feeling structure and let us inhabit it anew as the current image is placed within the context of its emotional precedents. Dreams have a special relation to waking reality and, as Bert O. States says in his analysis of dream structure: "We use them much as we use maps to find our way through the terrain of waking reality. Maps do not resemble the reality they refer to; but we are not surprised by this fact when we arrive at the place to which they have directed us" (States 1993: 9–10). Dreams act as an emotional map which places the current experience within the realm of past like experiences to encompass an amalgam of similar events into an overall feeling structure. States continues:

> Moreover, dreams gravitate toward base-level emotions: fear, anger, desire, embarrassment, sadness, guilt, or, simply, frustration – trying to do something that, for some unspecified reason, has to be done against a resistant world. One might say that dreams worry or ramify the emotion by giving it a representational structure made of things that are personally associated with the emotion.

> (States 1993: 92)

The same could be said about Bausch's pieces. They too tend to deal with base-level emotions and work with the ramifications of those emotions within experience. In approaching the broad range of human emotions by exploring them within the context of experience, Bausch is able to call upon particular, personal moments to explore deep structures that affect our own behavior and way of being in the world. In *Kontakthof*, the base emotion is our experience of the need for connection, and the underlying feeling we have as we enter into those patterns of behavior in our life where that desire for connection is a motivating factor.

The building blocks of Bausch's pieces are her images, but images not simply as visually crafted moments. For Bausch images act as patterns of experience, as ways of being in the world, not simply

visual information. The image of the couple undressing across the vast space, for instance, has contained within it feelings of desire, risk, and vulnerability. Of course we have never engaged in that precise action, but it enacts the same process by which we tentatively uncover ourselves in our own attempts at connection. The moment is particular, but uses that particularity as a referent to larger themes. It acts as a metaphor, structuring our own experience by creating a condensed version of what we feel at particular moments in our own lives. We enter the moment on stage empathetically, feeling the vulnerability of the couple and relating it to our own experience.

In Bausch's work, images exist for themselves. We are intended not to see beyond them, but merely to see them, or to see because of them. The things are themselves, they don't necessarily directly refer to something else, but in being themselves they are caught in a web of meaning and reference. They are not naive or pure, but stained with the vitality of experience that is necessarily in the world, and bring with them the history of their context. As such, each image relies on context, the flow of information, so that it becomes difficult to talk about images without talking about the way those images are pieced together, and it is just as difficult to talk about the organizing structure, the form that propels the piece, without talking about individual images, for they are both born of the same stuff. They both draw their life not just from a feeling but from a feeling structure, a deeper imprint of how a feeling works. The image does not evoke a specific feeling but is derived from the feeling itself to create a web in which we become enmeshed.

The image provides the ground by which we might come to know similar experiences in our lives, while attending to the actuality of the event as presented. As States says about the dream, "The dream image does not arouse feeling; it is instead the feeling that arouses the image, which is so deeply saturated in the feeling that it is impossible to distinguish one from the other" (States 1988: 47). The undressing couple does not express desire and vulnerability; the image gives us desire and vulnerability incarnate. The event is saturated with the feeling which stands as its base. It is a full moment, and has already included in it a sense of connection and forward motion. It begs the question of its relation to the images before it and we anticipate succeeding images in our attempts to derive meaning out of the whole. The image appears strange as an isolated moment, disconnected from

the context that heightens its affective potential, because it loses its imaginal base as one facet of a larger experience. And yet the image has a completeness of its own, containing within it the core of the whole from which it is drawn. In Bausch's pieces we place each image in the context of those surrounding it and within the context of similar events we have experienced in order to try to come to terms with an overall feeling for the piece, even as that feeling is contained within the image. The image lives in context and draws the context within its own walls.

Kontakthof works along these dream structures, creating an under-lying feeling in which we are enveloped. Rather than asking what the piece means, I am forced to acknowledge what it does. On Bausch's stage, the world is constructed through the constant interplay of the created world, the metaphoric implications of the events within that world, and the reality of the people as they are engaged in an act of presentation. The structure doesn't just mirror a dream; it utilizes the same expressive units and modes of engagement that our dream world contains. Like dreams, the images I see are sometimes absurd, some-times seemingly nonsensical, but they are invested with a quality that feels potent. As events and images unfold on Bausch's stage, they coalesce and knock me off my center. They do something.

CREDITS

All quotes and descriptions are drawn from repeated viewings of a production of *Kontakthof* presented at BAM in October 1985 as part of the Next Wave Festival. I have also drawn from a video-taped version of the piece currently held in the Dance Collection of the Lincoln Center Library for the Performing Arts. The piece premiered in Wuppertal on December 9, 1978, with the following credits: Kontakthof, Piece: Pina Bausch. Music: Charlie Chaplin, Anton Karas, Juan Llossas, Nino Rota, Jean Sibelius, and others. Collaboration: Rolf Borzik, Marion Cito, Hans Pop. Stage and costumes: Rolf Borzik. Cast: Arnaldo Alvarez, Gary Austin Crocker, Fernando Cortizo, Elizabeth Clarke, Josephine Anne Endicott, Lütz Forster, John Griffin, Silvia Kesselheim, Ed Kortlandt, Luis P. Layag, Maria DiLena, Beatrice Libonati, Anne Martin, Jan Minarik, Vivienne Newport, Arthur Rosenfeld, Monika Sagon, Heinz Samm, Meryl Tankard, Christian Trouillas.

PRACTICAL EXERCISES

SETTING THE STAGE

Pina Bausch's choreographic process began as a means to an end, a simple way to create something for herself to dance. In creating that first piece and her early work in general, she drew on her experience; from the German expressionist roots handed down through her mentor Kurt Jooss to the psychologically dynamic balletic tradition in which she was immersed with Antony Tudor. Bausch had encountered other methodological approaches as well, particularly from the burgeoning experimental dance and theater scene she witnessed in New York in the early 1960s. But she didn't set out to create a new approach to performance or to specifically further or challenge an existing method, and so never worked to establish a new technique or define a new way of moving or enacting presence on stage.

As the focus of the work with her company shifted, the emphasis became how to approach new material utilizing her and her performers' experiences in a wide range of theater and dance practices. Those experiences are brought to bear on the material at hand, and the means by which she creates new performance pieces are embedded in a long and rigorous rehearsal and developmental process. She keeps that process mostly behind closed doors, but her privacy is more to allow her performers the safety they need to risk failing in

order to breach previous structures of work to arrive at something new and different, rather than any desire to keep her methods secret.

Still, defining working methods for Bausch is difficult, and comes more from interpolating backward from the pieces themselves into potential pathways of construction necessary to put those materials in place. Bausch has commented on that process in numerous interviews as well, and so by piecing together elements from both these sources, it is possible to uncover a working method for developing new performance.

Bausch doesn't offer any particular exercises or performance techniques to follow, but she does provide a base to derive more specific rehearsal strategies for generating new material and approaching established works. Methodology is always a process of adaptation. You take a bit from here and some chunks from there and mold them to fit your interests and your own particular context. Bausch's work in particular relies on drawing from the resources you have, and the primary resource is people.

One of Bausch's greatest assets in her own developmental process is the time to sort through myriad attempts at new staged images and a consistent company of highly trained performers, many of whom have been with her for years. Most of us don't have such luxuries, but exploring Bausch's methods can still open up productive resources for creating new work.

Bausch's performance practice is built on a process of uncovering connections to fundamental ideas and feelings. She draws on the experience, both personal and professional, of her company in working toward that essential base, and her creative genius lies in her ability to construct intricate and delicate webs of feeling from the connections she uncovers, utilizing the human resources of those around her.

PROCESS OVER PRODUCT

Bausch inverts the priorities of process and product in her rehearsals. Rather than striving toward some terminating end, Bausch concentrates on the getting there, how it is we arrive at the attitudes we have and how we express that striving in our everyday lives. Just as the rehearsal mirrors the process of probing the world to find our place in terms of and within it, the performance also mirrors the

process of the rehearsal, so that the audience can approach the piece from the same base of exploration from which the performers and choreographer started.

Concentrating on the process as opposed to the product has far-reaching effects which realign the very base from which Bausch's pieces begin. Ballet and modern dance both essentially work through techniques of movement, utilizing a form that might lead toward the expression of the practitioner's ideas. The technique and the message of the piece stand as separate entities with the former at the service of the latter. But the technique stands as a given, and the process becomes drawing on that technique in such a way that something might be expressed. Similarly, when working on a play, the attempt is usually to use the base structure the script provides as a means for uncovering the heart of the piece. The script is used as a tool by the director and actors to get at underlying ideas. Both of these processes are primarily directed at the final outcome of the performance itself.

Bausch's work, however, starts with a base of ideas and feelings, whether derived from an open-ended question posed in rehearsal, or a structured source from which the developmental process emerges. Once that exploratory process begins, it follows its own necessity. This is one reason why working in this way can be so time consuming, because you could keep working forever, always uncovering a new element of the question at hand. Bausch is known to keep working up to and often beyond what is listed as opening night, but the looming presence of that deadline, even if it is often soft in her case (another luxury most of us cannot afford), can be a very powerful motivating factor, and contributes to the generation and organization of material at least as strongly as any other resource brought into rehearsals. The end product is not denied, merely removed from the pinnacle of importance it usually maintains.

The real innovation of tanztheater lies here, in the realignment of priorities away from a language of expression leading to a final product toward a questioning of what needs to be expressed and the subsequent process of confrontation and discovery that takes place through rehearsals. As Richard Sikes states simply, "Bausch's contribution to dance is a process, not a product" (Sikes 1984: 53).

Bausch's work, therefore, provides no easy model to follow. Would-be interpreters must push through a rigorous process similar to that which Bausch herself employs. But the process necessitates an

individual viewpoint, so the work takes on the character of those who do it. This individual approach comes through in the viewing of the performance as well, where you bring your own world to the piece and see it from that vantage point. This is one reason Bausch often refuses to speak about the content of her pieces. As she says, "Everybody sees a different piece. Nobody can see the piece I see. I see all the details in the rehearsals, and people see only one performance. I can't explain what I see, but if I could, you would understand me, not the piece" (quoted in Stendahl 1996: 68–69). To work with Bausch's developmental process means to find your own way to do something on stage that has an effect. You may arrive at something similar or something wildly different, but that depends in large part on who you are and the world in which you are contained.

The finished piece is not pre-imagined as a goal toward which to strive, but comes out as the process of its making, and that process is exposed. So within the piece there are compromises, warring priorities that have been made a part of the very structure of the work. The importance is not so much what each element is, but how they are made to belong, the connecting tissue that holds the disparate elements together. In performance that tissue comes from the process of rehearsal, where variations are tried and elements eliminated until the piece emerges from the cacophony of thoughts and ideas, movements, and images that the initial queries suggested.

DANCE CONSTRUCTION AND THEATER IMAGES

Tanztheater, as the name implies, is a merging of dance and theater modes, but merely identifying the presence of more than one element in the production does not make it tanztheater. No matter how peacefully the components coexist in the more usual dance/theater paradigm, they are still essentially different, each bringing its own set of conditions and expectations to be fulfilled or thwarted at any particular instance. Tanztheater relies on the infection and co-optation of one form by another, fully utilizing both forms' representational potential so that they are fused into a cohesive whole.

Story ballets have always applied dance technique to theatrical form and structural principles to create a theatrical dance where theater and dance coexist more intimately than by simple juxtaposition. Bausch and other proponents of tanztheater invert the scenario,

applying theatrical developmental strategies to what is essentially a dance structure of bodily engagement and expression. Bausch uses principles of dance construction and theatrical methods to explore an issue, and the audience is let in on the exploration. Rather than using those methods to tell the audience something, she creates an open metaphor for the audience to complete.

Bausch uncovers the very heart of the process of dance, the motivating impulse from which movement begins, and that impulse is always a person in a specific situation. The piece as performed becomes the arrangement of those moments as discovered in rehearsal from the performers' own experience and presented within physical and dramatic terms.

Bausch's challenge and great innovation was to find a way to maintain a dance agenda through choreographic principles of construction while incorporating theatrical techniques of expressing individual subjective experience. The expressive element is reoriented to be a real person in a real event. As Meryl Tankard recalled her response to the questioning mode of her audition for the company, "It was the first time a director had encouraged me to project my own personality on the stage, and it opened a whole new world, I had nothing against being a sylph in a tutu and toe-shoes, but the whole classical repertory suddenly seemed like a museum" (quoted in Galloway 1984: 41). It is this revelation of subjective experience in Bausch's pieces – derived from and represented through the performer's body – that is the basis for tanztheater and that provides the point at which dance and theater come together to form tanztheater.

Beyond utilizing any given performer's specific dance or theater training, Bausch's process asks for a realignment of how that training is considered. Dance moves beyond the intricate presentation of evocative movement, and theater steps around the illusory creation of a world on stage to engage the way in which performers are present.

Of course dance training has long moved beyond pure movement values (even if it remains a dominant influence, especially in America), and the theater world is full of challenges to the structures of illusion, but Bausch's work realigns the entire process and creates a world of presence that exists through the performer's body. Built into conventional models of theater and dance is the expectation we have to look past the reality of the performer on stage to see either that

performer's investment in character and a created world in theater, or the expressive potential of movement in dance. Those models create a presence of absence, where we are asked to look beyond the actual individual to the created expressive structure beneath. In Bausch, theatrical images that engage real presence are created in rehearsal and structured through dance principles to create a theater of bodily presence. The exercises that follow are all geared toward uncovering that process of engagement and bringing out the essential elements that cohere in Bausch's individual pieces and in the breadth of her work.

RECONFIGURING PRESENCE

Bausch's pieces create a world of immediate presence that directly engages the audience, rather than a re-presented world that comes from a constructed idea of time and space. These initial exercises are designed to set up a ground of interaction and presentation that helps the performer to enter into that dynamic relationship of direct presence.

ENTERING INTO TIME AND SPACE

The introductory exercises listed here establish a ground in simple presence in time and space. They help to enforce ideas of open response to allow performers to find points of interaction and connection from each other. Once the ground is set, performers have a base within which to place the more evocative images that further exercises are designed to evoke.

Exercise 1: Grid Work

▶ Set up a square on stage, with each corner a comfortable eight paces apart. Divide the entire group into four roughly equivalent smaller groups and have each group start at each corner of the grid. I find it helpful to work with music with a strong four-beat rhythm to start. The first set of four performers each set out from the four corners and enter the grid, walking in time to the music along the following pathway: 1. Across, 2. Down, 3. Diagonally back, 4. Down the other side, 5. Across, and 6. Diagonally back again.

▶ Each leg of the journey should take eight paces, and it is more important to maintain the eight-pace structure than to hit the exact points on the grid. Obviously, the diagonal leg is longer, and performers should adapt their steps to fit the greater distance. For people starting at alternate corners, merely rotate

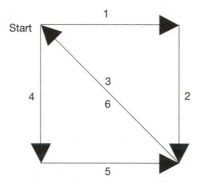

the diagram so that the starting point corresponds to their starting corner. In all cases, the pattern remains: over, down, diagonally back, and then mirror that on the other side. The walk should be simple and straightforward along the given pathways. Make sure that performers stay on the beat and the basic structure is maintained.

Establishing this basic pattern gives the performers an incredibly useful structure to help build awareness and response in space and time. The parameters are versatile enough to allow for response, but limited enough to keep people focused. Once everyone is comfortable with the basic structure, you can add in other parameters.

Exercise 1A: Continued Grid Work

▶ Once that basic structure is established, people can enter or exit into the space on their own, but always beginning at the start and leaving at the end of an eight count. Performers need to stay focused on what the active space needs, entering when the space demands and leaving when it feels appropriate. Simply being aware of the dynamic of the group within creates an alive tension in the performance space.

▶ Keep the walk simple and begin to notice other people in the space, someone whom you walk with, or walk parallel to for a time. The center becomes a meeting point that you have to negotiate in order to keep to your path. Let relationships develop as you feel the dynamic tension that is created at individual moments, but simply through a look or facial expression. Try to let the constrictions of the space itself create interactive possibilities rather than trying to force something to happen.

Giving performers a structure with limited variables opens them up to be able to respond to the subtlety of actual conditions in space and time. The goal is to create an open structure of awareness that allows for possibilities to develop as variables are added. Response comes from the conditions present in the active performance space and performers stay connected to that active potential even as they are outside of the arena.

Exercise 1B: Felt Response

▶ Once that basic awareness is in place, performers can adjust their walk based on felt response. Stay in time to the music, but you could walk double time or half time, or with small syncopations to move about the space. Be careful that it doesn't just become juking to the music, but that your walks come from and feed back into the dynamic of the group. Take time to stay outside the square to see what develops inside the performance space. Feel when it is appropriate to enter back in to the performance.

By using an exercise like this grid work to develop response on stage, performance presence shifts from the attempt to create a language of expression directed out to an audience to creating an arena of action that asks an audience in. That was a condition of performance I had responded to in seeing both theater and dance, but analyzing Bausch's work gave me the means to understand how to achieve it. Performers in Bausch's pieces create stage images, but they are always engaged in the present and open that response to an audience. Rather than creating a present moment out of a constructed time and space, they are present more immediately (and usually bodily).

The basic grid structure provides the resources to explore this dynamic and build awareness within it. You can also work more specifically with space or time and bring the performers' growing awareness of the way they exist in time and space back to the grid as you add more and more parameters.

Exercise 2: Relationship in Space

▶ Working in groups of three to start, and expanding to five or more (odd numbers help to mix up the group and prevent people from partnering up, losing touch with the overall stage dynamic), have the performers simply spread out in

space. Imagine the air between you as a fluid substance and any movement toward or away compresses or expands the space between you. Start with simple movements of the body concentrating on the space between individual performers.

▶ As the performers become attuned to the spatial tensions between people, allow actions to become broader, moving away or coming toward each other. Give yourself the chance to respond and once you make a move, give your partners a chance to react to the new dynamic within the group. Once you are comfortable with the dynamics of changing relationships in space through this active awareness of the space between you, you can work within the system, moving more fluidly and forcefully to alter conditions and react in time. Bring this awareness back to the grid to help develop response out of spatial dynamics.

Exercise 3: Relationship in Time

▶ Again working with three people to start and expanding as the group gets comfortable with response in time, have the performers simply walk about the space in straight lines, changing directions when they encounter someone else in the space. On a clap from outside the performance area, the performers all stop, and on another clap, they begin walking again. Stay attuned to the dynamics of the group in these moments of stillness and then as the walking begins again. Ask the performers to work to find those moments of stillness on their own, stopping and starting based on felt response among the group.

▶ Once the group is able to achieve this felt response in time, find ways to include it in different combinations, so that one person stopping may be connected to another while a third keeps moving, or one person simply stops amidst the activity of the rest of the group. Play with the different dynamics, keeping focus on how they alter the fluid relationships that are developed in the group. Add time and stillness into the elements of response in the grid.

The Viewpoints – created by Mary Overlie out of roots in dance practice and further developed by Anne Bogart, Tina Landau, and SITI Company – provide a thorough means of exploring and utilizing spatial and temporal awareness in performance. Bogart and Landau expand on the original viewpoints established by Overlie to include four distinct viewpoints of time (tempo, duration, kinesthetic response, and repetition) and five viewpoints of space (shape, gesture, architecture, spatial relationship, and topography). Performers work to keep an open awareness of their individual action, their

connection to others, and the overall group dynamic along these parameters of space and time. Training in Viewpoints can provide a more thorough structure for engaging performance presence in dance or theater (or combinations therein), but even these simple exercises can help to open up awareness and begin work from a base in real experience.

Once performers are comfortable with the grid structure, you can add more and more parameters, including more challenging music. Ask the performers to allow the music to enter in to their response without dictating action. Both varying and more complicated rhythmic structures, and stories within music can provide conditions of response guided by music. Bausch explores all manner of music in her rehearsal process, with an eye not simply to the feeling of the music, but to the cultural weight a particular song may have, and the ways in which performers can work with and against the music to achieve different effects. The structure of the grid provides a means to experiment with how different music creates different conditions on stage.

RELATIONSHIP TO AUDIENCE

Much of Bausch's work explores a direct connection to the audience. Even through the opening confrontational stare in a piece like *Kontakthof*, the barrier between the supposedly anonymous audience sitting in the dark and the created world of the stage in which we are asked to invest is broken. Just as we are made aware of the reality of the performed space itself, we are also often made aware of our role in the event, even if it is merely as witness or voyeur to what is put in front of us. These simple exercises are designed to open performer response to an audience.

Exercise 4: Presence

▶ This exercise is best performed in a large space, preferably a theater with a specifically designated audience area. Have a group of performers line up all the way upstage facing the back wall, their backs to the audience. Using peripheral awareness, walk backwards in unison at a slow pace and gradually lifting your arms and finally extending through your body to go up on your toes throughout the walk. Using the spatial awareness developed in the previous

exercise, focus on the condensing space between you as a unit and the audience. Let that energy be what buoys your arms up as you move toward the other side of the stage. By the time you reach the opposite edge of the stage you should have arrived at the full height of your extension. (Have a prompter help to ensure they don't fall off the edge of the stage.)

▶ As you stop, turn in unison, still on your toes and with arms raised above your head. Lower your heels to the floor and gradually lower your arms while looking directly out at the audience. Imagine the activated space between yourself and the audience and maintain that awareness as you now take the directed energy and bring it to a spatial or time exercise like the ones listed above.

The audience becomes another factor in the performers' structure of awareness, and continued work with exercises like this can help them to fill that space between the audience and the performance. The invisible boundary between the audience and the performance is permeated, allowing for a more direct communication between spectator and event.

Exercise 5: Interaction

▶ Two performers stand at a distance from each other and maintain eye contact. They work to feel the space between them, moving back and forth exploring the dynamic tension of space. Once a connection is made, one performer simply assumes a posture and facial expression expressing a specific emotion, trying to radiate that feeling across the space to his or her partner. Anger and defiance are easier to achieve than love or tenderness, but work with a variety of emotions switching back and forth to get a sense of what carries.

▶ Next have one person enter the performance space and assume a similar emotional stance, this time trying to express that connection to an audience. Remember, it's not charades, so the challenge is to create a dynamic connection based simply on activating the space, rather than doing something that the audience may get. After the first person has assumed a dynamic emotional stance, others join him or her so that the group gradually grows, all working to achieve that dynamic connection with the audience.

Conventional acting exercises often work with various means of maintaining a charged presence between performers, but it is generally something looked in on by an audience, and dancers work in partners and groups to create relationships among themselves and in space and time,

but they are often closed off to an audience. Methods like Contact Improv are wholly centered on creating an intimacy of connection between performers as a private act, wholly separate from an audience. A Bausch performance opens up that relationship between performer and audience in any number of ways. Sometimes, they literally break the bounds of the stage/audience divide: serving tea to the audience, coming down to the front row of the audience to share family photos, or even instructing the entire audience in a gesture sequence that leads us to hug each other. But outside of these overt interactions lies a more implicit direct relationship with the audience in the way in which we are included in the space and time of the performed moment and the way in which that boundary is continually transgressed.

ESSENTIAL ELEMENTS

Bausch's performance practice is created with fundamental building blocks that rely on the actual people engaged in the event, even as they construct a performing persona. Those individuals work through their own experience to develop theatrical images and movement/physical constructions. To build on that individual base, Bausch asks questions and gives her performers the freedom to respond in different ways: through words, a performed image, or a movement phrase. Each response comes from the individuals themselves, and draws on their own skills and abilities, history, and experience.

ASKING QUESTIONS

As we saw in Chapter 2, Bausch has always stated that the shift she made from technique-based rehearsal processes to more open-ended explorations came through asking questions. The questions may lead to stories from the performers or performed moments, but in either case what Bausch concentrates on, and what leads to usable material for performance, is the performers' connection to the prompt. The questions Bausch poses are aimed at the central feeling or idea that stands as the base of the developmental process for each piece, but questions often may approach that central focus more obliquely, and in fact, it is often through the process of asking and answering questions in rehearsal that a real underlying current begins to emerge.

In the earlier pieces, Bausch drew more heavily on her performers' own pasts, memories from their childhoods or particular experiences they may have had with love or loss. The residency pieces that Bausch has concentrated on for the last twenty years came with a ready base of the location itself, but once a feeling for the place began to emerge, then the questions might become more pointed and push toward individual experience. In *Nur Du* (1996), for instance, based on the company's residency in the American West, after the ensemble repeatedly discovered images of display and false fronts in their experience of Los Angeles, Bausch pushed them to consider times in their own lives when they were put on display. By concentrating on individual experience, but pushing toward the underlying structure of the feeling that goes with the experience, Bausch begins to create metaphoric images that speak to something more human in us all. The questions may move toward the personal, but because the images that result work to uncover the base structure of the experience, they become more universal. The moments as performed provide a wedge into the interior landscape of collective experience.

In *1980: A Piece by Pina Bausch*, a piece primarily about loss and derived at least in part in response to Rolf Borzik's death, Bausch uses clichéd formalities both for their literal value, with the attendant uncomfortableness that often surrounds them, and for their metaphoric relation to the larger theme. At one point a single woman is confronted by a large, tightly packed group. The idea of outsideness is simply and powerfully expressed as the performers stand in silence for a moment and look at the one woman cast out from the collective group. One at a time people leave the group and face the woman directly, offering rather flat recitations of tired departure lines, and then circle around and return to the group:

> "Goodbye, and a lot of success."
>
> "It's a pity that you have to go so soon, best regards."
>
> "Please don't forget us here, we'll be thinking of you."
>
> "What, you have to go! Oh, stay another five minutes. No? Oh well."
>
> "My dear, what a pity, it's not really time yet is it? Well then, all the best. Bye."
>
> "Bye, shall I see you to the door, and my best regards to your family. Everything's going to be just fine."
>
> "It's so wonderful to have met you. Take care of yourself."

When everyone has offered their farewell, the whole group waves to the woman who remains motionless. The image then dissolves into another. This scene is repeated in the second act exactly as it was performed in the first, except without words.

The cultural construction of goodbyes is examined to find the truth of loss and discomfort implicit in the situation, while simultaneously exposing the artificiality of the scene. The moment is derived from a simple question in rehearsal about a time you said goodbye. The answers, or phrases, the performers come up with in response all appear innocuous enough, but the context in which they are placed in performance makes the feeling of loss palpable. The act of leaving is brought to its metaphoric base and, even if derived from a particular context within the ensemble, is open to any moment of loss we have experienced.

Exploring something like love can be hugely daunting. Simply asking "What is your experience of love?" may lead to an outpouring of ideas, or just freeze people with the enormity of the potential response. Focusing questions at specific moments of the major idea in question can help to start uncovering the base structure for the experience as it is felt by individual performers. Asking them when they have found themselves in a moment of fear, or a sudden impulse of love, or afraid for their life, helps to activate the response by tying it to direct actions. Once those individual moments are on the table, then you can work to explore those ideas through a series of further questions and tasks to uncover the base structure of the feeling and use that to create stage images. I provide one example here of starting from questioning a direct experience, and then exploring the dimensions of that experience through a variety of means, but any number of prompts can begin the process.

Exercise 6: Getting at the Essence

▶ Describe a crisis moment in a love relationship. It can be a moment of transition in a romantic relationship, difficulty with a parent, brother, or sister, or simply a flare up in any relationship that is more emotionally intimate. Make sure that the moment you describe is specific.

  1 Write down the moment you describe and read it to the group.
  2 Have someone else read your story aloud.

3　Working in pairs, imagine yourself in the moment and re-create the physical structure of it; what you actually did in the moment. Switch places and re-create your partner's moment.

4　Combine your story with another pair's physical structure and vice versa.

Once you start exploring a simple question like this, you can tear it apart in any number of ways, then put it back together in varying combinations. Try different attitudes in performing the moment, from deadpan to energized. A heightened moment like this reveals the ways in which we are connected to each other, and any given individual's story begins to uncover deeper structures for how love and intimacy work and how we function in relation to them.

Reconfiguring an experience and presenting it in different form can also work toward uncovering the base structure of an image, opening up what may be a personal experience to a more universal attitude. In *Palermo, Palermo* (1989), Nazareth Panadero strides purposefully on stage with a sheaf of pasta under her arm. She looks directly at the audience and forcefully says: "This is my spaghetti. It's all mine. You can't have any and I won't give you any, it's mine, all mine." Holding up a single piece of pasta, she says: "You see this? Mine. And this? Mine too. I won't give you any, you can't have any. It is mine, all mine." She goes on in this vein for a good minute until her ownership of the pasta is unquestioned. She has endowed it with meaning and purpose. The moment is funny, but there is something desperate about her claims of ownership.

Panadero created this image out of her experience in Palermo and seeing the older women's sense of propriety and fierce loyalty to their own, whether it be family, house, or the town itself. Panadero performs this moment toward the beginning of the piece, and we don't see this "character" again. Once an image is presented, the performers often move on to images and other "characters" in creating the intricate collage of elements that make up a piece, but much later in the work Dominique Mercy coolly and calmly walks on stage, a sheaf of pasta under his arm. He looks out at the audience with a sly grin, delicately takes a piece of pasta out and breaks it. He does this again and again as he makes his way across the stage, all the while looking directly at us, implicating us in the act. The force of Panadero's ownership of that pasta makes Mercy's act one of extreme violence, and we are included in the act. The image is derived from a simple question of experience brought down to its essence and endowed with

special presence and then reconfigured to create a new image that continues and builds on the previous, furthering the web of meaning that the piece creates. Again, I provide one example here for working with this kind of prompt or question, but using different issues leads toward a range of material for performance.

Exercise 7: Reconfiguration

▶ Have the performers bring in a precious object, something simple that has taken on more meaning for them through its history, and then tell the story of the object to the group.

▶ Once there are a number of stories to work with, set up a variety of improvisational scenes of simple interaction where the goal is to get something done: seduce someone on a date, get someone to leave you alone, convince them to buy something, and so on. The stories become your text, or the objects themselves can become tools to get something done. Work simply and try not to force the action, but let the objects or stories do the work for you. Work from your memory of a given person's story.

The goal of reconfiguring a personal moment, whether it is an experience, an object, or relationship, is to uncover the motivating impulse of the event itself and why it has become important to the performer. By concentrating on that base structure, personal connections are made more universal and lead to an open interpretation from the audience, who are now able to place their own experience in the context of the event.

Often, a question in rehearsal may lead to staged images more through how you meet the challenge of answering it. Leaving a question open to see how different performers approach the idea becomes another tactic for opening up to the broader structure of an experience, placing it within the specific community of the ensemble.

Exercise 8: History in Your Body

▶ How do you carry your history in your body? Show the group. You can begin by describing how something is contained in your body, but let the story affect your body so that your physical presence is implicated in the telling.

As questions become more prompts to action rather than descriptions of experience, they naturally lead into performed images and moments

that work toward the underlying base of an idea through metaphor. The way in which a specific question is answered is often built out of the elements that have been in the rehearsal room up to this point. Asking for a developed response can be a means of coalescing some of the energy that has been in the room, and leads to more concrete performance images.

DEVELOPING IMAGES

Simply providing a means for ensemble members to contribute thoughts and ideas to the developing palette of resources for the piece can create an ongoing source of material. I often reserve the last half hour of early rehearsals for show and tell. Performers, designers, writers, or anyone else in the room can bring in something and show it to the ensemble. It may be something simple like a song they think might be appropriate, or a piece of text, but as the rehearsal process continues and the underlying feeling structure for the piece begins to emerge, ensemble members may come up with a moment of performance they contribute to the event. If nothing else, this tactic keeps a series of images and ideas alive in the room. If the piece is derived from a more particular base, these sessions can be used to display research into the topic at hand.

Once material is out in the room, the difficulty comes in finding ways to incorporate it into the overall work and the exhausting period of editing material to begin to complete a structure in which the various materials cohere. The first step is taking raw material and pushing it into more concrete performance images to use as elements for the final work. Bausch integrates those performative images with more movement-based elements as well. I provide a few examples for creating images and movement that are more directly related to Bausch's own developmental approach here, but just as Bausch draws on her own and her performers' full range of experience in theater and more essentially dance, any new developed work should draw from the experience of the people in the room and take advantage of whatever resources are at hand in developing new material.

Exercise 9: Complete a Feeling

▶ As simply as possible, create a concrete expression of a feeling. Rather than showing me the feeling, help me to feel it. How do you contain loss, desire,

hope, or despair in a performative image? The image should take place in time (i.e., not a "snapshot"), but should be a moment, an individual evocation of the feeling in question, rather than a series of events that tell a story. Once you begin to develop an image, what is necessary to complete it, to fill it out and support it? Performers should feel free to work alone or in pairs or groups, as necessary.

While rehearsing for *Walzer* (1982), Bausch asked the company about the feeling you have when looking at a display in a natural history museum.

> In museums you can see where they collect animals, stuffed animals. You can see how they are preserved and how they stand there, the animals. Or with insects, how they mount them so that people can look at them. An ensemble member questions, Do you want us to put it into words? and Bausch responds, No, I want you to do it, or do it to someone. Sometimes when they are put on show, or mounted, there's a little bit of realism there. A little piece of the world they came from. A bit of meadow or whatever. I mean, it's different when they're just stuck on, that's OK somehow. But you get a real sense of it when you know it's been mounted with a pin. A pin gives a different sort of awareness because you know a pin hurts. Something like that, something very simple.

> (*Was Tun Pina Bausch und Ihrer Tänzer in Wuppertal*? 1983)

What Bausch is striving for here is a particular feeling of discomfort in looking at such things in a natural history museum. But rather than simply representing that experience, she asks the company to try to re-create that feeling. The image need not be a direct expression of that event, indeed, when a few ensemble members try to re-create the event of mounting someone to a wall, Bausch interrupts them and says that that's not it, it's too literal, it tells us about the feeling, but it doesn't give it to us. It is illustrative rather than evocative. The images do not mean or point directly to a particular circumstance; they attempt to capture the feeling pattern attendant with that experience and express it in individual terms that are joined into a deeper structure through an emotional connective. It is this connective to which we respond. What it means depends on who you ask and so it is not reducible to a particular interpretation. Bausch is not trying to create an experience where we may say: "Ah, I get it, it's like animals

in a natural history museum," because then either you get it or you don't, but in either case the image stops there, once the connection has been made. What she is trying to do is recapture the experience implicitly, to leave it open for whatever associations we, as onlookers, might choose to make. The feeling is connected to a larger goal, and the image is the feeling.

Exercise 10: From a Myth

▶ Create a singular performative image from a myth. Work with the essential base of the myth rather than telling the story. Uncover the base feeling of the myth and find a way to evoke that on stage. Make it interesting. Think about context, raising the stakes, details of production, the role of the audience. How can you take your basic idea and make it more visceral, more felt, more engaging, more interesting? No language except in a poetic, rather than literal vein. The whole piece should be a singular image, 30 seconds may be fine, and no more than 2 minutes. Condense, structure, develop, engage, and present.

Myths are often concretized images of complex feeling structures. For example, in the myth of Sisyphus, the story of a man rolling a rock up a hill is less important than the feeling structure that goes with it; a combination of struggle, persistence, and futility condensed to the point that it stands as a defining image. We know that feeling and can now call it simply Sisyphean. It is a metaphor that contains that experience, and this exercise asks the performer to create a new performance metaphor that captures the essence of the story at hand. This kind of image is essentially a further condensation of many of Bausch's pieces as a whole, moving from the story operas that worked to create new performance metaphors for complex structures like *Orpheus and Eurydice*, to the idea-based pieces, and finally the residency pieces that re-create the feeling structure of a location. But creating a simple image forces performers to rely on concrete theatrical elements, the human body in space and time, interaction with other people, real presence, heightened stakes, and so on.

Exercise 11: Do Something to Someone

▶ Working in pairs, each person develop a series of simple physical actions based on a routine. It may be preparing for bed, or making coffee in the morning. More

difficult, but potentially more interesting might be preparing to make a difficult phone call, responding to bad news, and so on. Once you are able to perform the actions, have the other person lead you through them, physically manipulating your body as if it were a full-scale mannequin.

Something happens to people when their physical agency is taken away and they are led through action rather then in charge of their own movements. Of course, to work in this way requires a certain level of co-operative effort from both the performers, the person being manipulated may appear lifeless, but is actually helping to achieve the action. The image that is created focuses an audience's attention on the elements of the action itself, rather than what they may indicate. Many of Bausch's pieces have small moments of one person acting for another, with the attendant feeling caught in the surrounding context.

DEVELOPING MOVEMENT

Because of Bausch's primary background in dance, many people look to her work for movement-generating ideas. Movement strategies are central to Bausch's work, with initial prompts more naturally derived from her performers' extensive background in dance practice. Especially in more recent pieces, movement-centered prompts are frequently interspersed amidst the more image-driven questions. She might ask her performers to dance their name, or to bring in a favorite song and create a dance to it. More specific movement strategies often come out of the gestural work described in detail in the next section, but there are some more basic movement-based structures Bausch adopts from her background in expressionist dance and particularly her work with Kurt Jooss.

Exercise 12: Respond to the Other Person

► Working in pairs, standing simply facing each other, one person initiates an action. The action should be simple, but come out of an impulse in relation to the other person: a turn of the head, a reach toward, moving to another point in the space, and so on. The other person takes in the first action, and responds with an action. Simply respond and try not to plan your action. Let the dialogue develop between the two people with alternating actions, stopping every four actions or so to repeat the phrase that is developing and then continue on. You

should build a repeatable series of actions, so keep going back as necessary to keep the sequence alive in your bodies.

▶ Keep building in this way, but let the actions become intertwined, closing up the time between action and response, until each person's actions become more fluid. Allow the actions to become interactive, touching the other person, grabbing his or her arm, etc., and then retreat or move apart again as necessary for the particular dialogue you create. Let the developing phrase take precedence over your original actions, so that if you need to adapt some actions to create a more fluid or more dynamic sequence, do so.

Exercise 13: Remove the Other Person

▶ Build a response phrase as described in Exercise 12. Remove the other person to create a solo phrase. Try doing both solo phrases apart, and then repeating them so that they finally cohere into the original two-person phrase you created. Where does the point of contact come? Try building the phrase with music. Add in music at varying points in the repetition and connection of the phrases.

Dialogue phrases like this can be manipulated along many different parameters to create both solo and partner work. You can begin with a simple feeling attached to the connection between the couple (love, fear, aggression, etc.) or imagine them as either general or specific relationships (mother and daughter, Romeo and Juliet, etc.). The movement comes out of direct response and becomes an evocation of more basic feeling structures. Once you are comfortable working with this level of response, you can find that response within yourself as you react to a specific idea or emotional state.

Exercise 14: Gestural Paths

▶ Create an emotive gesture based on a specific emotion. Let the gesture move in your body from its original expression to another part of your body, and then another, and another. Join the series of expressions from one part of your body to the other into a fluid and repeatable series of movements. You can keep building in this way, finding new expressions for the same base emotion and following their path through your body, or you can develop the emotional base to create a shifting pathway of expression. What does it do to your action to move from desire to want to need, for instance? Find the next emotional condition in a connected sequence and keep adding elements to your physical expression.

This kind of exercise is designed to create movement out of emotional states, and to work toward the complexity of most situations where such emotions are at play. Physical responses to emotional conditions start from a recognized base in simple action, but take on a more full intent through extenuation. The base for this kind of work comes from expressionist dance practice of the 1920s, but Bausch has used resources like this in creating everything from the large choric work in early pieces like her seminal *Rite of Spring* (1975) to more individual work in recent pieces like *Ten Chi* (2004) or *Vollmund* (2006).

LOOKING FOR ACTION

What people do on Bausch's stage is often intensely physical, but not necessarily derived from organized movement patterns. She creates arenas for action, and works through strategies for engaging physical presence as it is situated in context. Gesture becomes a potent tool in the inter-relationship between image and movement; showing how both come from an emotional and personal source and reflect common underlying feeling structures. Bausch's pieces and process provide a dynamic base for incorporating physical languages into developing new work, or for creating a physical base for characters in scenes from established plays.

GESTURE

Bausch's work with gestures is derived from German expressionist dance, and also incorporates the long-standing tradition of gestural work in expressionist and epic theater practice. Gesture is more inclusive than a simple movement, and becomes a complete action, often with underlying intent. This approach necessarily brings in dramatic potential, and operates along the lines of Bertolt Brecht's idea of *Gestus*. In German, *Geste* is more simply defined as "gesture," whereas *Gestus* incorporates a feeling that is more replete, more full of the intent from which the action derives. *Gestus* can be applied to things besides action as well, whenever something is filled with a spirit that delineates it. *Gebärde* is the word more often used in German to describe gesture in performance as a more complete action, and can even be used to describe the manner or conduct through which

behavior is exhibited. Gesture in Bausch's performance practice takes on this broader sense of behavioral and emotive expression.

The Viewpoints, as explained earlier, work with gesture as one parameter, breaking along two lines: behavioral gesture and emotive gesture (derived from the German *Ausdrucksgebärde*, or expressive gesture). The behavioral gesture is simply that which we do in life; running your hand through your hair, wringing your hands, etc. Emotive gestures take on the full intent of an emotional state and show us something more abstractly, as in placing your hand to your heart, etc.

While behavioral gestures may be revealing, especially when recontextualized as Bausch does with typically masculine or feminine gestures, their aim is not necessarily to project intent. Emotive gestures carry the energy of the underlying idea and often give it palpable form, helping us to feel a performer's intent rather than simply understand it.

Some emotive gestures have risen to the level of cliché, like holding your hands over your heart. Clichés can be good tools – there is a reason a simple action has come to be understood so directly – as long as you are careful not to get caught on the surface level of the gesture,

Figure 4.1 Gesture work in *Bandoneon* (1980). Photo by Bettina Stöß

using it to telegraph a specific idea rather than to uncover a deeper intent. If you play through the cliché to find the motivating impulse behind the action, the power behind the gesture can be put to use.

Exercise 15: Essential States

▶ Identify key words for the piece you are exploring and have each performer come up with a gesture based on those words, one gesture for every word. Stand in a circle and have each performer teach the others his or her gesture for the first word until everyone can do it. It may be helpful to adapt the gestures to a four count for ease in learning and to be able to replicate them. Once everyone has learned the gestures, perform them in an order to create a gesture sequence. Feel free to rearrange people in the circle to accommodate an easier flow from one gesture to the next in a sequence. Play music to provide a four-count structure and run through the gesture sequence in the circle.

Bausch often includes gesture sequences of this kind in her performances. Sometimes those sequences are based more on behavioral gestures and then are performed in unison as the group walks in time to music. It is a simple way to create movement patterns that are related to the expressive base of the material under consideration. Because people are devising their own gestures, there is no issue of someone's ability to do the physical action. It is already based on what they can do, whatever their training.

Exercise 16: Gesture Dialogue

▶ Once a gesture sequence has been established, revisit the individual gestures to create a gesture dialogue. Two people work with the gestures, improvising with them individually as a means of relating to each other. A gesture from one person is followed by another gesture from the other person. As with language in dialogue, it's not just the precise articulation of the gestures that matters, but the tone with which they are done. What would it mean to do the gesture quietly, or loudly? Imagine an internal volume dial that changes the expression and intensity of the gestures and try working with a dialogue at a setting of two or eight. Let the dialogue take the lead and let the gestures adapt to the needs of what happens. Performing this dialogue to music can help guide the exercise and provides a good structure on which to hang the gesture work.

Some of the gestures will keep coming up in dialogue because they are useful, and others will fall away because performers don't think of them in context. If it's not memorable, let it go. The nature of the work is such that you come up with a huge number of gestures anyway, so keep the ones that work and let the others slip away. Beginning with one pair performing and the rest of the ensemble watching helps to get a feel for the action, with a chance to stop and talk about what worked and what felt awkward. After everyone has had the chance to work with the gestures, the exercise can progress to larger open conversations, with everyone participating simultaneously.

As people work with the gestures in this way, some change is often required to adapt the gestures to the context that develops between performers. Sometimes, performers are reluctant to let go of the "right" way to perform the gestures, but encourage them to let the context push the gestures into what they need to be. Dancers in particular, I've found, have been drilled in getting a physical movement right, and often have difficulty making it their own or changing it to work with another person, while actors have a tendency to get sloppy and the expressive potential of the original gesture gets lost. A balance of structure and freedom provides a stable base.

Exercise 17: Interactive Gesture

▶ Once the ensemble is comfortable working with the gestures in dialogue, allow them to adapt them by doing them to each other (this may have happened already in the gesture dialogue). What happens to a gesture when it is done as a direct point of connection between two performers? Let the interactive gestures transform the dialogue as it develops to create a broader ground of interaction between two characters expressed through combinations of individual and interactive gestures.

Bausch often develops simple gestural expressions with her performers, but the way those gestures are done to one another creates much larger expressive metaphors. In an image from *Bluebeard* described in Chapter 1, for instance, a woman crouches on the floor behind a table at which the man playing Duke Bluebeard sits, passively looking out at the audience. We see her hand rise up and describe a tender path up the man's body toward his face, and just as she reaches the point of tenderly caressing him, he violently shoves her head back down to the

floor and out of sight, without moving his eyes from his distant goal. After a moment, we see the hand again and the action is repeated, again ending with a violent push to the floor. Again we see the hand rise up and the whole sequence is repeated several times, getting faster and faster until the woman finally stops, leaving the man to continue looking impassively at the audience. There is a moment of stillness before we see the hand rise up once more, only to be brutally rejected.

Here, the simple gestures of tenderness and violent rebuff are expanded, and repetition serves to shine new light on the image (see Exercise 19 on formal variation for a more specific discussion of repetition). The way in which the gestures are performed on someone else begins to define the relationship and its metaphoric connection to larger themes. We feel the intensity of the image in part because something real is happening to the woman, and even though we know the action has been carefully choreographed to minimize risk of actually hurting the woman, the violence is such that we flinch at each repeated push back down to the floor, and we are brought in to the world of the piece through interaction. Once those gestural images are in place, any further use or development of them in the piece becomes a gestural language that the characters can use and with which the audience is now familiar. Once a broad range of gestures has been explored, with different dynamic levels and as both individual actions and interactive elements, then the gesture language that is developed can be used more freely in varying combinations. Try creating a scene simply out of gestures, or applying the gestures to an existing scene from a play.

Bausch's pieces often employ extended gestural languages derived from the motivating impulse of the piece. In *Masurca Fogo* (1998), based on the company's residency in Lisbon, the piece is built on basic elements of their experience translated into physical gestures of connection and more fiery interaction. The embrace of an open, often sexual connection builds throughout the piece through this gestural language until it finally erupts into a party scene where the performers literally create a "Love Shack" out of boards while sensuously dancing to the B-52s' song of the same name.

Exercise 18: Gesture Relationship

▶ Working in pairs, create a four-gesture sequence that evokes the relationship between two people. Pay attention to the way in which person A's original

gesture leads to person B's next gesture, and how person A then responds, etc. After completing the four-gesture sequence, find a way to have the last gesture lead back in to the first, so that the sequence can be repeated.

Bausch continually returns to this pattern of gestural relationship and uses a variety of manipulative strategies to uncover underlying intent. In *Café Müller*, Malou Airaudo and Dominique Mercy establish a relationship as lovers (seemingly held apart by some circumstance). At one point in the piece, the two meet and slowly raise their arms into an embrace. Jan Minarik enters, gently takes Airaudo's hands off Mercy, then takes Mercy's hands off Airaudo, and places their faces together in a static kiss. Minarik then raises Mercy's arms up to a position bent 90 degrees at the elbow. He places Airaudo's arm around Mercy, lifts her, and places her in Mercy's arms so that she is lying limply on her back. Minarik leaves and Mercy slowly lets Airaudo drop to the floor. She bounces up to hug Mercy in the same position in which the scene started. Minarik, who had been walking out, hears the activity and slowly returns to reposition the couple in the pose in which he left them, methodically repeating his actions in the same sequence as before. He turns to leave again, Airaudo is dropped, returns to the embrace, Minarik returns, the couple is rearranged again, Minarik leaves, Airaudo is dropped, etc.

The action goes through several repetitions, getting faster and faster as the scene progresses. Finally Minarik leaves for good and the couple continues repeating the action, working up to a frantic pace until they stop in an embrace and we hear the sound of their breathing, heavy from the exertion. Airaudo slowly moves off to continue her path around the room and Mercy slowly exits. This couple meet on several other occasions throughout the piece and repeat the same series of actions before moving off in their own direction.

The relationship between these characters is expressed in a series of four interactive gestures: a hug, a kiss, the woman lying in the man's arms, and the woman dropped to the floor. When I saw this sequence, I connected it to *Romeo and Juliet*, where the embrace of the lovers is acted upon by an outside force to become the embrace of death, and even after the influence of the outside force has been removed, the pattern of behavior is set and so continues along its inevitable path.

The specific reference is unimportant, for what comes out is simply two people striving for connection, and the attempt is made palpable

through a manipulation of the relationship gestures performed in sequence. This gestural pattern helps to create the context of the image, even as it relies on that same context to help enforce its own potent expression. It is derived from the same base operative conditions that inform the rest of the piece and is woven into the structure as one part of the overall effect.

MANIPULATING FORMAL CONSTRAINTS

One of Bausch's most potent tools is the simplest: formal variation. Once images or gesture sequences are developed, Bausch tries any number of variations. But more than simply creating a new approach by doing any given action faster or slower, or repeating it, etc., Bausch looks for what the formal shifts lead to and how they reveal some other aspect of the base condition that was the motivating impulse for the piece itself. Repetition becomes a habitual pattern and a faster tempo moves a gentle image to a violent one. It is that new evocative heart which now becomes incorporated into the work.

Exercise 19: Formal Variation

▶ Once you establish gesture sequences or relationships as described above, you can further develop them through simple formal variation. Isolate a given element of the action and try different approaches along that parameter.

▶ *Distance*

Try repeating a gesture sequence or relationship from a great distance. Imagine that the other person is right in front of you, even as they are across the room. As the sequence repeats, you can gradually come together so that you finally meet in the middle, or one person can come to the other stationary figure, eventually joining him or her, and the previous isolated gestures become interactive.

▶ *Tempo*

Do the same thing moving from slow to fast, or vice versa. Try working in different time structures, so that one person moves quickly while the other moves slowly, or they cross paths as one moves from slow to quick and the other from quick to slow.

▶ Intensity

Try the gesture sequence at different levels of intensity or with people working at different levels, so that one person is always at a level of ten, while the other is at a level of two.

▶ Repetition

Find different patterns of repetition of a particular gesture or gesture sequence. Take advantage of what repetition allows, and adapt the sequence to fit the expression that results.

Changing formal constraints of a gesture sequence forces you to see it from a different perspective, and often a new level of expression is revealed. Bausch frequently uses combinations of these variations to create new effects. The embrace sequence described above gradually increases the tempo until the previously tender image becomes a desperate conditioned reflex. Similarly, in the moment from *Kontakthof* described in Chapter 3 where the performers gesture to each other from across the stage, and then the men gradually move toward the women until they are on top of them with their attempts at communication becoming flailing attacks, the image is built on a simple variation of distance and intensity.

The example from *Bluebeard* described above uses repetition to uncover underlying intent. The image's expression moves from a moment of compassion and cruelty to the ongoing pattern of cruelty and the persistence of desire to find connection even in that. The moment also moves from one of personal struggle between Duke Bluebeard and his wife to a more open connection to all moments of futility and persistence we may have been involved in ourselves. It becomes a metaphor through concentration on the underlying impulse of the gesture. The interactive gesture dialogue consists of just two words, endlessly repeated, and that serves as a means to feel the behavioral patterns we all find ourselves stuck in at certain points in our lives. The action subsumes the performers as characters, and they are lost within it, unconnected and unable to escape as the image begins to take on the possible outcome of its underlying meaning. It is not a moment in a linear story, but one expression of the fundamental feeling structure of the whole.

STRUCTURING

The feel of a Bausch piece comes as much from the structure of the work as from her reorientation of liveness of presence. The choice and placement, or the orchestration of elements on stage creates a collaged structure that reveals the underlying feeling of the piece. The pieces are all combinations of actions that create dense interrelated pathways of images built on a central idea or feeling. Rather than telling a linear story, with its attendant quality of resolution, Bausch's pieces employ a looser structure of exploration and held tension, so that they are literally texted (from the same root as textile), as different elements are woven into a whole. Sometimes the weave is fairly loose, but if you look long enough the overall texture of the fabric comes through. It is a subtle interlacing and juxtaposition of likenesses, because the focus of the work relates to the underlying feeling structures that stand as the base motivating impulse. In this way, the pieces are a making sense of an idea rather than a telling, and we are engaged in the process of feeling instead of being shown a feeling or idea.

Each piece is structured to discover feeling rather than to mean. The structure of exploration that Bausch utilizes to such astounding effect is one of montage. Scenes are linked through more open points of relevance, without the necessity of plot or consistent character to draw the audience along. This allows the audience to find their own personal entrance points into the work, and then to exist within the intricate layering of images and movements that create the overall effect of the piece. The combinative network of actions creates a field of reference surrounding a particular feeling. You set yourself within this structure and approach it from your own vantage point. Rather than passively receiving information from your seat in the darkened house, Bausch's structures demand active participation to discern your relation to the underlying feeling of the piece.

Bausch builds systems of awarenesses. It is not just what each successive image says about the underlying structure, but how they infect and affect each other, creating a web of sense. This texting takes place both through the progression of the piece and in the simultaneity of some of the stage action. Images occur in reaction to other images, sometimes overlapping and sometimes separate. The resulting piece is so richly textured that we cannot contain it in our head as an instance of projected meaning. The pieces are felt more than they are understood.

Bausch asks a question on the first day of rehearsal and the answer is the piece, with all of the weight of the exploration contained in the discovery.

Narrative, or story, becomes a process of engagement that often comes out of the density of images and the ways in which they come together. Specific exercises are hard to describe because this structuring process is a part of the overall creation of the work, and takes on more importance toward the end of the developmental process utilizing elements generated during rehearsals. We can, however, talk about general strategies and ways of using them.

Exercise 20: Layering

▶ Create a list of elements that might be involved in the piece. If you are developing a new piece, this can come from the base idea that motivates the work, and if you are working from a singular source, list resources that respond to the feeling of the piece in question. Think about what objects might be in this world, what music, any text or stories, other media, relevant pictures or images, lists or non-fiction sources, and so on. As you develop images in rehearsal, you can put them back into your original list, categorizing each element of the piece.

▶ Once you have elements laid out in a list, pull from the various categories and try adding elements together to create a layered stage image. On a simple level, this can mean trying this song with this image, but you can also add more and more layers to create more evocative moments on stage. Also consider putting seemingly disparate things together; the tension that results from two dissimilar actions happening simultaneously can be potent as well.

Exercise 21: Dislocation

▶ Take a performed image developed within the context of the rehearsal and remove it completely from its original context, or place it within an entirely new context. For instance, use a movement phrase derived from a relationship or list of key words as a means of relating to someone else in an entirely different moment in the piece.

▶ Take the time to let the original moment rub against this new world, and then let the friction created help to transform both the original resource and the new context to which it is brought.

The most important aspect of this type of reworking material is to listen to what the work tells you. It is easy to get stuck in an original

context and not see the potential within created moments to extend into other areas of the piece. By staying alert to the evocative potential of any given moment, Bausch is able to draw the most from each idea and each performer. In the pasta moment described above, for instance, Dominique Mercy is able to redirect the original intent of the founding image and use it to extend the conditions of the entire piece, without lessening the intensity of the initial moment as performed.

Exercise 22: Densing

▶ Take two individual moments created in rehearsal and merge them together. Rather than simply layering one on top of the other, think of what needs to happen to allow one image to take on the other, so that they both are transformed to become a third image, related to the first two, but with its own intent and potential.

In *Nefes* (2003), a small Indian woman comes onstage and performs an intricate, gestural movement phrase that incorporates both elements of Western modern dance technique and traditional Indian dance. By incorporating both of those evocative structures, Bausch has already created a dense image that carries significant weight within the piece. After she has finished, a man enters, sits in a chair, his back to the audience, and asks the woman to do it again. The woman demurs, but the man insists, and both he and we are now witness to the same movement phrase repeated. The man makes it clear that she is now doing this solo for him (and for us), and we see it in a different light. The movement is beautiful, and in part I was happy to have the chance to see this solo again. But I am made aware of my own use of the dancer in this way, and feel a bit guilty. Of course the original phrase was done for me too, presented so that I might take it in and find something in it – enjoyment, meaning? – the options don't matter, but it does matter that I place myself in a position of receiver and look to the dance to give me something. Now that the process of creation and reception are made clear, I am left to question my own relationship to the event. That questioning comes out of the structure of the piece itself, and this particular moment is built on layering, dislocation, and densing, all combined together.

Finally, once a wealth of material is created, you can open a structure that brings together the performers' open awareness of the stage

space and each other with the elements that define the piece being developed. Performers now have the resources to be openly creative from within the piece, creating new material that helps them further flesh out the world.

Exercise 23: Open Play

▶ Toward the end of the rehearsal period, gather up all of the resources that are going into the piece to date. Simply allow the performers to move through the elements of the piece and find new juxtapositions of familiar elements. Use any music that is a part of the piece and play it in a different order than it is used in the piece. Take any props and provide access to them for the performers to use at any given time. Performers can use any text that is included in the piece, in any form. Make sure to take time to participate in the world that develops and time to step out and watch, always remaining alert to what the developing world needs and how you can contribute, or back away to let things happen.

Here again, listening is all-important, keeping an open awareness during the work to be able to jump in as the developing world demands something. The elements of the piece itself will dictate the world, but performers are now free to move within that world in a different way. They have any number of resources on which to draw, but can play within the world in a more free way, letting new discoveries happen. I often actively DJ the event, trying to use the music as a means to both spur action and respond to what is developing. I also leave a pad and pen out and ask performers to take a moment to write down anything they see that strikes their interest. It often takes quite a while for performers to open up to this kind of improvisation, but once they do, remarkable things can happen. Even after some good images or moments come out of the work, let it keep going. After a lull, you may find a new level of engagement as the performers exhaust predictable responses and start to let things happen.

Even if no new stage images are unearthed, giving the performers the opportunity to play within the created world of the piece gives them a new sense of freedom and commitment to the work when you return back to the structured world of the performance as you have articulated it. The piece is returned to the immediacy of the moment, and you are able to rediscover the motivating impulse of many of the moments you have created in rehearsal.

Bringing that sense of open awareness and response to the performance creates the feeling of being witness to an event. The most potent difference I felt in watching Bausch's work for the first time was the sense of a dramatically charged physical presence created out of the reality of people in space and time, their connection to the audience, and the way in which action is structured to lead us into the world on stage. Gesture and response provide a physical ground of presence on stage that accounts for the real time and space of the performers. They are necessarily fully engaged in the moment as it develops rather than projecting themselves into a created sense of other, in either character or articulated movement. The structure of the piece works to uncover that presence rather than lead us through a linear narrative toward some desired end. We are placed in the midst of an action that takes place in its own time and space. It is that sense of something really happening on Bausch's stage that has opened up dance practice to become more than movement for movement's sake, and provides a physical base in experience for theatrical process. To follow that process is to draw on what Bausch can teach us about the nature of performance.

BIBLIOGRAPHY

Adolphe, Jean-Marc. 2007. "Corpus Pina Bausch." *Pina Bausch*. Heidelberg: Editions Braus, 9–24.

Aloff, Mindy. 1987. "Two Continents: Two Approaches to Dance." *BAM Next Wave Festival Souvenir Program*, 64–73.

"Bausch, Pina." 1986. *Current Biography*. September: 3–6.

Bausch, Pina. 1975. "Choreografin Pina Bausch über ihre Arbeit." Interview with Edmund Gleede. *Ballett-Jahrbuch des Friedrich Verlags*.

—— 1978. "Not How People Move but What Moves Them." Interview with Jochen Schmidt, 9 November. In *Pina Bausch Wuppertal Dance Theater or the Art of Training a Goldfish*. Cologne: Ballett-Bühnen-Verlag, 1984: 227–30.

—— 1982a. "My Pieces Grow From the Inside Out." Interview with Jochen Schmidt, 26 November. In *Pina Bausch Wuppertal Dance Theater or the Art of Training a Goldfish*. Cologne: Ballett-Bühnen-Verlag, 1984: 234–37.

—— 1982b. "The Things We Discover for Ourselves Are the Most Important." Interview with Jochen Schmidt, 21 April. In *Pina Bausch Wuppertal Dance Theater or the Art of Training a Goldfish*. Cologne: Ballett-Bühnen-Verlag, 1984: 231–33.

—— 1983a. "I'm Still Inquisitive." Interview with Jocen Schmidt, 23 December. In *Pina Bausch Wuppertal Dance Theater or the Art of Training a Goldfish*. Cologne: Ballett-Bühnen-Verlag, 1984: 238–39.

—— 1983b. "Pina Bausch: an Interview by Jochen Schmidt." *Ballett International*. Vol. 6, no. 2. February: 12–15.

—— 1985. "'I Pick My Dancers as People' Pina Bausch Discusses Her Work With Wuppertal Dance Theatre." Interview with Glenn Loney. *On the Next Wave*. October: 14–19.

—— 1989. "The Evolution of Pina Bausch." Interview with Sylvie de Nussac. *World Press Review: Le Monde*. October: 91.

—— 1992. "Come Dance with Me." Inteview with Nadine Meisner. *Dance and Dancers*. Sept/Oct: 12–16.

—— 1994. "Gespräch mit Pina Bausch im Goethe-Institut Paris." Interview with Dr. Ros. Transcription by Susanne Marten. Goethe Institut, Paris.

—— 1995. "'You Have to Keep Totally Alert, Sensitive, Receptive': Pina Bausch Talks with Norbert Servos." *Ballett International/Tanz Aktuell*. December: 36–39.

—— 1998. "Zu extrem, um nachahmen zu können." Unlisted Interviewer. *GI-Intern*. 3: 19–21.

—— 1999. "Every Day a Discovery … " Interview with Christopher Bowen. *Stagebill: Cal Performances*. October: 10C–11A.

—— 2004a. "Ich glaube nur, was ich gesehen habe." Interview with Ulrich Deuter, Andresas Wilink. *K. West*. October: 5–10.

—— 2004b. "Pina Bausch über Lust." Interview with Eva-Elisabeth Fischer. *Süddeutsche Zeitung*. Nr. 223, 25/26 September: 8–12.

—— 2007. "'Man weiß gar nict, wo die Phantasie einen hintreibt': Ein Gespräch mit Pina Bausch gefürt von Jean-Mark Adolfe." *Pina Bausch*. Heidelberg: Editions Braus, 25–39.

Baxman, Inge. 1990. "Dance Theatre: Rebellion of the Body, Theatre of Images and an Inquiry into the Sense of the Senses." *Ballett International*. Vol. 13, no. 10. January: 55–60.

Bentivoglio, Leonetta. 1985. "Dance of the Present, Art of the Future." *Ballett International.* Vol. 8, no. 12. December: 24–28.

Bentivoglio, Leonetta and Francesco Carbone. 2007. *Pina Bausch oder Die Kunst über Nelken zu tanzen.* Frankfurt am Main: Suhrkamp.

Blom, Lynne Anne, and L. Tarin Chaplin. 1982. *The Intimate Act of Choreography.* Pittsburgh: University of Pittsburgh Press.

Bowen, Christopher. 1999. "Pina Wears the Pants." *The Times.* January 19: C1–2.

Borzik, Rolf. 1980. *Rolf Borzik und das Tanztheater.* Wuppertal: Tanztheater Wuppertal Pina Bausch GmbH.

Breslauer, Jan. 1996. "Open-Eyed in L.A." *Los Angeles Times.* March 17: 3–4.

Buchwald, Karlheinz. 2007. "If I Tried Concentrating on Getting My Arm Right, Then My Feet Went Wrong." *Kontakthof with Ladies and Gentlemen over "65."* Paris: L'Arche: 30–35.

Chamier, Ille. 1979. *Setz Dich Hin und Lächle: Tanztheater von Pina Bausch.* Cologne: Prometh.

Climenhaga, Royd. 1997. "Pina Bausch, Tanztheater Wuppertal in a Newly Commissioned Piece: *Nur Du (Only You)."* *TPQ.* July: 288–98.

Cody, Gabrielle. 1999. "Woman, Man, Dog, Tree: Two Decades of Intimate and Monumental Bodies in Pina Bausch's Tanztheater." *TDR.* August: 115–31.

Copeland, Roger and Marshall Cohen. 1983. *What is Dance?* Oxford: Oxford University Press.

Daly, Ann, ed. 1986. "Tanztheater: The Thrill of the Lynch Mob or the Rage of Woman?" *TDR.* Spring: 46–56.

—— 1996. "Pina Bausch Goes West to Prospect for Imagery." *New York Times.* September 22: 10–20

Delahaye, Guy. 2007. *Pina Bausch.* Heidelberg: Editions Braus.

Dixon, Michael Bigelow and Joel A. Smith, eds. 1995. *Anne Bogart: Viewpoints.* Lyme, NH: Smith and Kraus.

Fernandes, Ciane. 2001. *Pina Bausch and the Wuppertal Dance Theater: The Aesthetics of Repetition and Transformation.* New York: Peter Lang Publishing.

Finkel, Anita. 1991. "Gunsmoke." *The New Dance Review.* Vol. 4, no. 2. October–December: 3–10.

Fischer, Eva Elizabeth. 1998. "Reflections of the Times: The Inter- and Multimedia of Tanztheater." *Tanztheater Today: Thirty Years of German Dance.* Exhibition Catalogue. Seelze/Hanover: Kallmeyeresche, in association with Ballett International/Tanz Aktuell.

Foreman, Richard. 1995. "From Unbalancing Acts (1992)." *Twentieth Century Theatre: A Sourcebook.* Ed. Richard Drain. London: Routledge, 68–74.

Galloway, David. 1984. "The Stage as Crossroads: Germany's Pina Bausch." *In Performance.* Vol 13, no. 6. March/April: 39–42.

Hoffman, Eva. 1994. "Pina Bausch: Catching Intuitions on the Wing." *New York Times.* September 11: H, Section 2, 12.

Hoghe, Raimond. 1980. "The Theatre of Pina Bausch." *The Drama Review.* Trans. Stephen Tree. T-85: 63–74.

Kaufmann, Ursula. 1998. *Nur Du: Ursula Kaufmann Fotografiert Pina Bausch und das Tanztheater Wuppertal.* Wuppertal: Verlag Müller und Busmann.

——— 2002. *Ursula Kaufmann Fotografiert Pina Bausch und das Tanztheater Wuppertal.* Wuppertal: Verlag Müller und Busmann.

——— 2005. *Getanzte Augenblicke: Ursula Kaufmann Fotografiert Pina Bausch und das Tanztheater Wuppertal.* Wuppertal: Verlag Müller und Busmann.

Kerkhoven, Marianne van. 1991. "The Weight of Time." *Ballett International.* Vol. 14, no. 2. February: 63–68.

Kirchman, Kay. 1994. "The Totality of the Body: An Essay on Pina Bausch's Aesthetic." *Ballett International/Tanz Aktuell.* May: 37–43.

Klemola, Timo. 1991. "Dance and Embodiment." *Ballett International.* Vol. 14, no. 1. January: 71–80.

Klett, Renate. 1984. "In Rehearsal with Pina Bausch." *Heresies.* Vol. 5, no. 1: 13–16.

Koegler, Hörst. 1979. "Tanztheater Wuppertal." *Dance Magazine.* February: 51–58.

Kozel, Susan. 1993/4. "Bausch and Phenomenology." *Dance Now.* Vol. 2, no. 4. Winter: 49–54.

Lawson, Valerie. 2000. "Pina, Queen of the Deep." *Sydney Morning Herald*. July 17: 18–19.

Lelli, Sylvia. 1999. *Körper und Raum: Pina Bausch, Reinhild Hoffmann, Susanne Linke, William Forsythe, 1979–1999*. Wuppertal: Verlag Müller und Busmann.

Mackrell, Judith. 1999. "The Agony and the Ecstasy." *Guardian*. January 21: C1.

Manning, Susan Allene. 1986. "An American Perspective on Tanztheater." *TDR*. Spring: 57–79.

—— 1993. *Ecstasy and the Demon: Feminism and Nationalism in the Dances of Mary Wigman*. Berkeley: University of California Press.

Manning, Susan and Melissa Benson. 1986. "Interrupted Continuities: Modern Dance in Germany." *TDR*. Spring: 30–45.

Manuel, Diane. 1999. "German Choreographer Pina Bausch in Rehearsal." News Release. Palo Alto, CA: Stanford University, October 20.

Meisner, Nadine. 1992. "Come Dance With Me." *Dance and Dancers*. Sept/Oct: 12–16.

Müller, Hedwig and Norbert Servos. 1986. "Expressionism? 'Ausdruckstanz' and the New Dance Theatre in Germany." *Festival International de Nouvelle Danse, Montreal, Souvenir Program*. Trans. Michael Vensky-Stalling, 10–15.

Partsch-Bergsohn, Isa. 1987. "Dance Theatre from Rudolph Laban to Pina Bausch." *Dance Theatre Journal*. October: 37–39.

Partsch-Bergsohn, Isa and Harold Bergsohn. 2003. *The Makers of Modern Dance in Germany: Rudolf Laban, Mary Wigman, Kurt Jooss*. Hightstown, NJ: Princeton Book Company.

Pina Bausch: In Search of Dance. Documentary Film.

Pina Bausch: One Day Pina Asked ... Documentary Film. Dir. Chantal Ackerman. Bravo International Films, 1984. 40 minutes.

Regitz, Hartmut. 1998. "Beyond the Mainstream: Everything Else You Find in Tanztheater." *Tanztheater Today: Thirty Years of German Dance*. Exhibition Catalogue. Seelze/Hanover: Kallmeyeresche, in association with Ballett International/Tanz Aktuell.

Robertson, Allen. 1984. "Close Encounters: Pina Bausch's Radical Tanztheater is a World Where Art and Life are Inextricably Interwoven." *Ballet News*. Vol. 5, no. 12. June: 10–14.

Schlicher, Susanne. 1987. *Tanztheater*. Reinbek bei Hamburg: Rowohlts.

—— 1993. "The West German Dance Theatre: Paths from the Twenties to the Present." *Choreography and Dance*. Vol. 3, part 2: 25–43.

Schmidt, Jochen. 1984. "Pina Bausch: A Constant Annoyance." In *Pina Bausch Wuppertal Dance Theater or the Art of Training a Goldfish*. Cologne: Ballett-Bühnen-Verlag, 13–16.

—— 1985. "Pina Bausch and the New German Tanztheater: Movement from the Inside Out." *Festival des Nouvelle Danse, Montreal, Souvenir Program*, 59–65.

—— 1990. "The Wuppertal Choreographer Pina Bausch – The Mother Courage of Modern Dance – Turns Fifty." *Ballett International*. Vol. 13, no. 6–7. June/July: 40–43.

—— 1994. "From Isadora to Pina: The Renewal of the Human Image in Dance." *Ballett International/Tanz Aktuell*. May: 34–36.

—— 1998. "Learning What Moves People: Thirty Years of Tanztheater in Germany." *Tanztheater Today: Thirty Years of German Dance*. Exhibition Catalogue. Seelze/Hanover: Kallmeyeresche, in association with Ballett International/Tanz Aktuell.

Schulze-Reuber, Rika. 2005. *Das Tanztheater Pina Bausch: Speigel der Gesellschaft*, with photographs by Jochen Viehoff. Frankfurt am Main: R.G. Fischer.

The Search for Dance: Pina Bauch's Theatre with a Difference. Documentary Video. Script Direction, Patricia Corboud. Bonn: Inter Nationes, 1994. 28 min.

Servos, Norbert. 1981. "The Emancipation of Dance: Pina Bausch and the Wuppertal Dance Theater." Trans. Peter Harris and Pia Kleber. *Modern Drama*. Vol. 22, no. 4: 435–47.

—— 1984. *Pina Bausch Wuppertal Dance Theater or the Art of Training a Goldfish*. Cologne: Ballett-Bühnen-Verlag.

—— 1985. "On the Seduction of Angels." *Ballett International*. Vol. 8, no. 12. December: 72–76.

—— 1996. *Pina Bausch – Wuppertaler Tanztheater oder die Kunst, einen Goldfisch zu Dressieren.* Kallmeyer: Seelze – Velber.

—— 2003. *Pina Bausch: Tanztheater.* Photographs by Gert Weigelt. Munich: K. Kieser.

Sikes, Richard. 1984. "'But is it Dance … ?'" *Dance Magazine.* June: 50–53.

Smith, Amanda. 1984. "New York City." *Dance Magazine.* September: 35–37.

States, Bert O. 1985. *Great Reckonings in Little Rooms: On the Phenomenology of the Theater.* Berkeley, CA: University of California Press.

—— 1988. *The Rhetoric of Dreams.* Ithaca, NY: Cornell University Press.

—— 1993. *Dreams and Storytelling.* Ithaca, NY: Cornell University Press.

Stendahl, Renate. 1996. "Pioneer Dance." *San Francisco Focus.* October: 66–70.

Tanzland Nordrhein-Westfalen. 1999. Special promotional publication. Cologne: Ministry of Employment, Social Issues and City Development, Culture and Sports of the State of North Rhine Westphalia Office of Public Affairs in association with the NRW State Office for Dance.

"Tanztheater." 1989. Unpublished transcript, October 28. Sp. Lincoln Center Library for the Performing Arts, New York. Participants: Reinhild Hoffmann, Susanne Linke, Susan Manning, Susanne Schlicher, Marcia Siegle. Moderated by Madeline Nichols.

Tanztheater Today: Thirty Years of German Dance. 1998. Exhibition Catalogue. Seelze/Hanover: Kallmeyeresche, in association with Ballett International/ Tanz Aktuell.

"Thoughts on the Creation of *Nur Du* and Bausch's World." 1996. *The University of Texas College of Fine Arts Performing Arts Center Program*, Pina Bausch Tanztheater Wuppertal – Bass Concert Hall, 22 October.

Viehof, Jochen. 2000. *Pina Bausch: Ein Fest.* Wuppertal: Verlag Müller und Busmann.

Warren, Larry. 1991. *Anna Sokolow: The Rebellious Spirit.* Princeton: Dance Horizons.

Was Tun Pina Bausch und Ihrer Tänzer in Wuppertal? Videocassette. Dir. Klaus Wildenhahn. Inter Nationes, 1983. 60 minutes.

Wehle, Philippa. 1984. "Pina Bausch's Tanztheater – A Place of Difficult Encounter." *Women and Performance.* Vol. 1, no. 2. Winter: 25–36.

"What the Critics Say." 1986. *TDR.* Spring: 80–84.

Wigman, Mary. 1975. "Creation." *The Mary Wigman Book: Her Writings.* Ed. and trans. by Walter Sorell. Middleton, CT: Wesleyan University Press, 85–96.

Williams, Faynia. 1997. "Working with Pina Bausch: A Conversation with Tanztheater Wuppertal." *TheatreForum.* Winter/Spring: 74–78.

INDEX

Note: Page numbers in **bold** refer to figures.

Related titles from Routledge

Mary Wigman
Routledge Performance Practitioners series
Mary Anne Santos Newhall

All books in the **Routledge Performance Practitioners** series are carefully designed to enable the reader to understand the work of a key practitioner. They provide the first step towards critical understanding and a springboard for further study for students on twentieth-century performance, contemporary theater and theater history courses.

A dancer, teacher and choreographer, Mary Wigman was a leading innovator in expressionist dance. Her radical explorations of movement and dance theory are credited with expanding the scope of dance as a theatrical art in her native Germany and beyond.

This book combines for the first time:

- a full account of Wigman's life and work
- a detailed discussion of her aesthetic theories, including the use of space as an "invisible partner" and the transcendent nature of performance
- a commentary on her key works, including *Hexentantz* and *The Seven Dances of Life*
- an extensive collection of practical exercises designed to provide an understanding of Wigman's choreographic principles and her uniquely immersive approach to dance.

ISBN13: 978-0-415-37526-9 (hbk)
ISBN13: 978-0-415-37527-6 (pbk)
ISBN13: 978-0-203-09898-1 (ebk)

Available at all good bookshops
For ordering and further information please visit:
www.routledge.com

Related titles from Routledge

Robert Lepage
Routledge Performance Practitioners series
Aleksandar Saša Dundjerović

All books in the **Routledge Performance Practitioners** series are carefully designed to enable the reader to understand the work of a key practitioner. They provide the first step towards critical understanding and a springboard for further study for students on twentieth-century performance, contemporary theater and theater history courses.

Robert Lepage is one of Canada's most foremost playwrights and directors. His company, *Ex Machina*, has toured to international acclaim and he has leant his talents to areas as diverse as opera, concert tours, acting and installation art. His most celebrated work blends acute personal narratives with bold global themes.

This is the first book to combine:

* an overview of the key phases in Lepage's life and career
* an examination of the key questions pertinent to his work
* a discussion of *The Dragons Trilogy* as a paradigm of his working methods
* a variety of practical exercises designed to give an insight into Lepage's creative process.

ISBN13: 978-0-415-37519-1 (hbk)
ISBN13: 978-0-415-37520-7 (pbk)
ISBN13: 978-0-203-09897-4 (ebk)

Available at all good bookshops
For ordering and further information please visit:
www.routledge.com

Related titles from Routledge

Bertolt Brecht
Routledge Performance Practitioners series
Meg Mumford

All books in the **Routledge Performance Practitioners** series are carefully designed to enable the reader to understand the work of a key practitioner. They provide the first step towards critical understanding and a springboard for further study for students on twentieth-century performance, contemporary theater and theater history courses.

Bertolt Brecht is amongst the world's most profound contributors to the theory and practice of theater. His methods of collective experimentation and his unique framing of the theatrical event as a forum for aesthetic and political change continue to have a significant impact on the work of performance practitioners, critics and teachers alike.

This is the first book to combine:

- an overview of the key periods in Brecht's life and work
- a clear explanation of his key theories, including the renowned ideas of Gestus and Verfremdung
- an account of his groundbreaking 1954 production of *The Caucasian Chalk Circle*
- an in-depth analysis of Brecht's practical exercises and rehearsal methods.

ISBN13: 978-0-415-37508-5 (hbk)
ISBN13: 978-0-415-37509-2 (pbk)
ISBN13: 978-0-203-88210-8 (ebk)

Available at all good bookshops
For ordering and further information please visit:
www.routledge.com